Invest in Your Life: Why Wall Street wants YOU

✦

Everything You Need to Know About Investing in Your Life Insurance Policy

Ronald M. Roth, CLU, ChFC

iUniverse, Inc.

New York   Bloomington

Invest in Your Life: Why Wall Street wants YOU
Everything You Need to Know About Investing in Your Life Insurance Policy

iUniverse books may be ordered through booksellers or by contacting:

iUniverse
1663 Liberty Drive
Bloomington, IN 47403
www.iuniverse.com
1-800-Authors (1-800-288-4677)

ISBN: 978-0-595-49430-9 (pbk)
ISBN: 978-0-595-49243-5 (cloth)
ISBN: 978-0-595-61097-6 (ebk)

Printed in the United States of America
iUniverse rev. 3/10/09

For My Son Zachary

Contents

Acknowledgements

I would like to express my love, thanks, and deepest appreciation to Claudia for her unconditional love, support, and encouragement. To my parents Geri and Barry Roth for their never ending confidence in my work and their initial readings of the developing manuscript. Their insight and advice was invaluable to the success of this project; to Gary, Cindi, and Jacob Roth who are always in my heart and are part of my inspiration; to the entire Spataro family who have welcomed me and Z into their lives and for whom I have the utmost respect and love for; to the rest of my "Core Four" Michael, Steve, and Billy and their families who are close to me in ways only they can know; to my Ex-Comm, Adam, Rob, and Jeffrey who have become some of my closest friends and confidants; to Erik Mallon whose commitment to this project and experience in the publishing industry has been so very important to its success; to Eric Tannenbaum for his significant contribution to our business and spiritual growth; to our associates James Smith, Brian Edelman, Richard Brier, Ron Givens, Scott McVicker, Herb Feldman, and Grace Prowoski; to my new friends in Israel and Europe who have taught me there is more to life then meets the eye and the importance in realizing it; to our stellar business relationships including Mark and Mike at Universal in Florida and Henry, Steve and Mark that makes Phoenix a special place for us; a special thanks to my ex-partner Steve Wechsler who taught me how to think big and who has always been a very special friend.

Preface

Maybe you've heard the pitch …

"Psst! You! Yeah, you! We've got a deal for you. How about two years' free life insurance? Sound good? It gets better … We'll give you a cruise, too. Or a car. Or maybe, just maybe, a big, fat check, say, for $30,000? And you don't have to pay for a thing. Not one penny out of your pocket. All you have to do is sign a few papers, transfer your life insurance policy over to us, and—presto!—you've got a cruise to the Caribbean. Or a Bentley. Or that plump check. Whaddya say?"

If you're like most people, you're probably thinking that this sounds too good to be true. Nothing in life is ever this easy. Our parents taught us that there is no such thing as a free lunch, and this seems an awful lot like the sort of thing they were warning us about. That's what I thought, too, once upon a time. But you know what the punch line is?

It's real.

All of it.

Absolutely, shockingly real.

Okay, so let's say you're one of the increasing numbers of folks who knows someone who has done one of these deals. They got their cruise, their car, their nice, big check. They seem pretty darn happy with it, too.

What if I told you that they got hustled? And not in the way you might think. That check didn't bounce. That cruise was, indeed, very pleasant. There was nothing wrong with the Bentley they got. No, the reason they got hustled wasn't because there was anything shady or wrong … they got exactly what was offered.

The problem is, they could have gotten more. Maybe even a lot more.

Instead of a cruise or a car or a even a check for $30,000, imagine receiving a check for $200,000. Or $300,000. Or more. Sometimes, much more.

We'll teach you how.

Whether or not you have heard of these deals, whether or not you currently own a life insurance policy, whether or not you are familiar with the basic concepts of life insurance, the following pages will give you everything you need to know to turn a life insurance policy into a sound, safe, substantially profitable investment. Our goal is to demystify the entire process from beginning to end. We want you to understand every step of the deal, who profits, how it works, and what the potential risks are. We don't really believe in secrets. We want to pull back the curtain to show you the inner workings of what we do.

By the time you have finished reading through the pages that follow, you will know more about the life insurance market than many who work in the industry. Armed with that knowledge, you can make the choices that are best for you, not those that are best for investors or brokers. After all, it's your insurance policy, shouldn't you be the one who profits most when you invest in your life?

1

Introduction

I remember when I first heard about the notion of selling one's life insurance policy as a genuine form of investment. It was a sunny but somewhat brisk day in the fall of 2003, and I was just settling into a brand new office space. I was sitting at my desk, still organizing some of those odds and ends that always need organizing right after an office move, when the phone rang. On the other end was a nice, soft-spoken gentleman from California. After we made our introductions, we got down to the reason for his call. It was, in a word, a question, and his question went something like this:

"I've just heard of a deal where I can get free life insurance for two years. After those two years are up, I can either keep the policy by paying for it or elect to sell it for a profit. They tell me I won't ever owe any money unless I buy the policy, even if everything goes south on the deal. Is it possible that this is legitimate?"

In my fifteen years in the industry, I had never heard of such a deal before. My initial reaction was a bit like that of the gentleman on the phone; it just seemed too good to be true. I did find myself intrigued by the possibilities, however, so I offered to look into it.

Little did I know that what I would find would send my career hurtling headlong into a new world of unexplored opportunity.

Prior to that phone call, our business focused exclusively on the marketing and distribution of high-end insurance estate planning through CPA firms. We had been very successful at this and were quite content with the space we had carved out in the insurance industry. But as I dug deeper into the secrets of the emerging life insurance market, I found the roots of a burgeoning industry just beginning to grab hold. The way of thinking about life insurance was changing. Old ideas were turning upside down. Big things were happening. I knew I had found a market that was just about ready to explode, and of course I wanted us to be a part of it.

So we learned about life settlements, the life insurance secondary market, non-recourse premium financing … all the terms and concepts we'll help you understand in the following pages. And as we learned, we began to find our place in this nascent industry. We continued in our capacity as insurance brokers, but we also called on our experience in estate planning to help us serve as advisors to our clients in this new life settlement market. We found ourselves acting as gatekeepers, connecting our clients and those investors on Wall Street who were desperate to get a piece of these promising investment opportunities.

Within six months, we were working on more cases than we could imagine, and we were still just learning the process. It was only the beginning. We had gotten in early, and we were in for quite a ride.

Yet even as the industry grew and we became more successful within it, I couldn't help but be reminded of an impression I had right at the very beginning: If big-time investors are so willing to snap up these policies, surely our clients could get more out of the deal than the comparably small upfront payments they were receiving. After three years of working in the industry, I discovered that my initial impression was correct. Each "layer" in the investment chain was just stripping more profit away from the client. I knew we could do better.

The Invest in Your Life strategy was born.

2

Life Insurance 101: The Crash Course

Originally, this is where we had a history of life insurance. It had material about Asia Minor and ancient Romans. It had a long section about 16th century English sea captains. We figured every book about insurance could use lots of stuff about sea captains.

Then we cut it all out.

Know why?

Because it was a history of life insurance.

Perhaps there are less exciting things to read about than life insurance history, but we can't imagine what those are.

Furthermore, we suspect that you're not reading this to learn about the history of life insurance. We suspect you're reading this because you would either like to discover the most profitable way to sell your life insurance policy or are looking for the best means for securing your loved ones' financial future. There really isn't a whole lot about life insurance that you absolutely need to know to do these things. However, there are basic concepts and terms that are important, and we want to make sure you are comfortable with these before we move into the somewhat more complex subject matter you will find later in this book.

To help us illustrate some very simple concepts, we are going to use one little piece of life insurance history. We'll keep it short. We promise. It'll hardly even hurt ...

Learning the Basics with William Gybbons
(or The One Tiny Little Piece of Life Insurance History We Decided to Keep in this Book)

William Gybbons was not a sea captain. He was a salter, which apparently means he put salt on food for a living. He lived in London, England in 1583. None of this is even remotely relevant.

What is relevant is that his life was worth a little less than 400 British pounds.

On June 18, 1583, the first modern-style life insurance policy ever recorded was taken out on Mr. Gybbons' life. In effect, it was nothing short of a bet. The specifics of the policy were that a fellow by the name of Richard Martin paid £30 to a collective group of sixteen London merchants as a wager that Mr. William Gybbons, Londoner and salter, would die sometime during the following year. If Mr. Gybbons lived out the year, Mr. Martin would lose the £30 he paid; if Mr. Gybbons passed away, the merchants would pay Mr. Martin the precise sum of £383.6.8. If you are wondering how we know all this, it is, amazingly, still maintained as an official matter of record in the Chamber of Assurances archives in the Royal Exchange of London. That is high-quality record-keeping.

We're going to use the case of Mr. Gybbons to introduce the basic terminology you'll see when dealing with a life insurance policy today. We know that many of you already have life insurance. Many more are already familiar with life insurance terminology. If this is the case for you, we're going to ask that you bear with us for just a bit while we get the rest of the class up to speed.

If you're someone who doesn't know a single darn thing about life insurance, don't worry … that's why we're here. We know there's nothing worse than some goofball describing something you don't really understand using terminology you don't really know. It happens every time we talk to our computer guys. We'll do our level best to keep it simple here.

So … putting the above wager in today's insurance policy terms would go something like this …

The £30 Richard Martin paid would be the policy's *premium*. A premium is a regular payment paid to insurers as the cost of purchasing a policy. These payments must be paid faithfully in order to keep a policy *in force*, or active. For life insurance policies, premiums are often expressed in annual terms, so the annual premium for this contract was £30.

Insurance contracts consist of three parties: the insurer, the insured, and the policy owner. In this example, the sixteen merchants are our *insurers*, and William Gybbons is our *insured*. The *policy owner*, also called the *policyholder*, is Richard Martin, because he took out the policy on Mr. Gybbons' life, and he paid the premium. It is often the case that a policy's owner and the person it insures are the same person; usually a person takes out a policy on their own life and pays the premiums themselves. For this reason, you will sometimes notice both in this book and elsewhere that the terms "policyholder" and "insured person" are used interchangeably. However, it's important to note that, as in this case, a policy's owner does not always have to be the person insured by that policy. There is a distinction.

Richard Martin only paid one annual premium because the duration of the coverage was for only one year. Some life insurance policies terminate like this after a period of time that is set in that policy's contract. The length of time for which coverage is provided is called the policy's *term*, and insurance coverage with an expiration date is called, cleverly enough, *term insurance*. After the term is up, the policyholder must choose whether they want to renew the coverage or not. If renewal is desired, the policyholder will have to sign up for a new term. Insurance coverage without an expiration date is called *permanent insurance*. There are different types of permanent insurance, but we'll get into all that in the next chapter.

Okay … so back to Mr. Gybbons, Londoner and salter extraordinaire. As you recall, if Mr. Gybbons dies during that year of coverage, our friend Richard Martin gets £383.6.8. In a current-day contract, that £383.6.8 would be called the *benefit*. By definition, a benefit is the payout an insurance company has to make when a policy *matures*, that is, when the conditions set forth in a coverage contract have been met. In this case, the benefit would have to be paid if Mr. Gybbons passes away within a year. When you hear someone talking about the *face value* of a life insurance policy, what they are referring to is the amount of the assigned death benefit, i.e. a policy that is "worth $10 million" is a policy with a $10 million death benefit.

In most kinds of insurance, any claim benefit is paid directly to the policyholder. That's obviously not the case for life insurance. Since those insured by life insurance will have passed away in order for the benefit to be paid, it's unlikely that they're going to do much shopping. Instead, the policy owner designates the people or organizations to whom the benefit will be paid in the event of the insured person's passing. These designees are called the policy *beneficiaries*. In the Gybbons contract, Richard Martin is both the beneficiary and the policy's owner.

Summarizing, then, in the language of today's insurance-speak, the Gybbons contract is a one-year term policy worth £383.6.8 with an annual premium of £30 and a single assigned beneficiary, Richard Martin, who also happens to be the policy's owner.

Now I bet you just won't be able to sleep tonight unless you know how Richard Martin made out in this little wager. As it turned out, William Gybbons sadly did indeed pass away the following year. Doubly unfortunate was the fact that he happened to pass away exactly 364 days after the policy was signed into effect. The merchants who had offered the policy then tried to avoid paying the claim by arguing that a "year"—by their definition— actually consisted of twelve months, each in turn consisting of four weeks, thus a "year"—by their definition—was actually only 48 weeks long. Richard Martin was unimpressed by this reasoning. He took his claim to the Appeal Court, who had the good sense to rule in his favor and grant him his benefit.

It is thus the regrettable legacy of poor Mr. William Gybbons that he should be the object of not only the first modern life insurance policy, but also of the first claim refusal, the first claim grievance, the first life insurance court ruling, and the first all around life insurance mess. We wish we could tell you that this sort of thing absolutely never happens anymore. The problem is that the instant anything requires legal boundaries, there will be ambiguities, disputes, courtroom wrangling, and general grumpiness. Just remember that the next time you hear of an insurance company denying a claim. All they're really doing is paying respectful homage to a tradition that is at least four and a quarter centuries old. That's how we like to think of it. We're very positive people.

So … What's So Great About Life Insurance?

Traditionally, people have bought life insurance because someone who relies on the policyholder will require some level of financial support in the event of the policyholder's death. To put it in a single word (or, actually, a single hyphenated compound word), the historical reasons to acquire life insurance have always been *need-based*. These tend to fall into one of three common categories:

- The policyholder pays a succession of premium payments to gain the assurance that a larger amount of money will be made available to his or her beneficiaries. This money will pay any personal debts, funeral expenses, or estate taxes that will need to be accounted for in the event of the policyholder's death. We like to think of this as the "don't stick my loved ones with the bill" philosophy.

- The policyholder is a household breadwinner and pays premiums so that his or her beneficiaries (usually a spouse or children) will have some level of financial security when the policyholder dies. If this happens while the policy is in force, the newly deceased policyholder's income is lost to the household, but the benefit paid out is substantial enough to enable the household to pay its expenses for a significant period of time. We call this the "let them remember me with extra fondness when they're buying themselves a new Lexus" plan.

- The third need-based reason is a little different than the other two. Imagine that there is a person who is extremely important to a company. Let's say he's a CEO named Svlad. Svlad is a company hero. He negotiated all the sales contracts; he's the mind behind the marketing; he knows where the decaffeinated coffee is. Now let's say Svlad dies suddenly while parachuting off the summit of Mount Everest during a mid-winter lightning storm. Our company is in a lot of trouble. They may lose some of those contracts. They will need to hire several people to perform all of the job functions that Svlad did himself. It will cost a lot of time and money to replace him. Now imagine that the company recognized the potential for this dilemma beforehand and so bought a life insurance policy on Svlad. In this policy, the company is both the owner and the beneficiary of the contract, and the benefit paid to the company when Svlad dies is designed to help it survive his loss long enough to recover. We'd like to say we have another witty little name for these sorts of arrangements, but the industry has already come up with an official, boring one: *key person contracts*.

Eventually, a whole new fourth reason to buy life insurance evolved. Unlike the three traditional objectives, this new reason wasn't need-based; it was investment-based. People already knew that their policies were a good investment for their heirs. But policyholders gradually came to realize that their policies could provide a significant rate of return during their own lifetimes, too. As we shall see over the course of this book, it took a while for folks to figure out the proper way to use their policy as an investment vehicle and there was a real choice to be made between holding and selling their policy. But when they did …

Well, let's just say things started getting interesting.

And profitable.

Really, really profitable.

The Case Against Life Insurance and Why It No Longer Applies

This all sounds just fine, you might be thinking, but you're still not sold. We think we have some idea as to why you might not be leaping at the chance to fork out money for those life insurance premiums.

For one thing, you may see life insurance as a liability cost, an undesirable, miserable, ugly step-child of an expense. You may really despise the notion of paying an insurance company for something you aren't required to have by law (like auto insurance), and you just don't want to spend that money on premiums when it could go toward a fancy trip to Rome. We understand that. We're not huge fans of spending money, either. And Rome is a pretty nice place. But as we'll show you in the coming pages, money spent on life insurance isn't just being swallowed up by a big hole never to be seen again. What you're actually buying when you purchase a life insurance policy is nothing less than an investment in biological real estate. And unlike the current real estate market in most parts of the country, biological real estate is positively booming. So when you pay those premiums, you're not throwing money away; you're investing. Looking at it in those terms will make it a lot easier when you dole out your money for those premiums. We'll be getting into the details of this investment process far more deeply throughout this book. For now, we just ask that you trust us. That policy is worth something.

Another thing you might be thinking is that you've "outgrown" your need for life insurance. Your household accounts have accumulated enough wealth to ensure the long-term financial security of your spouse. Your estate has grown large enough to handle death expenses like an estate tax or burial costs. As a parent, your children have grown up and are out on their own, so life insurance just doesn't seem necessary. Maybe your company has grown up too, and it has outgrown the need for a particular individual's key person contract. But to avoid life insurance for any of these reasons is to be stuck in old ways of thinking. Today, life insurance is as much an investment as it is an instrument of financial security. You can't outgrow the need for a good investment, because you can't outgrow the need for money. Heck, if anything, you only need more money as you get older. And if you do buy a life insurance policy, you just might find that you are happy to have it. Ultimately, you may want to hang onto it rather than sell it to investors. Wouldn't it be a good thing to give your loved ones a farewell present that you know they could use? A million bucks might be nice. They could buy themselves a new pair of shoes … and maybe a house to keep them in.

A third factor that holds people back from life insurance is the fact that it is, well, life insurance. The act of dying pretty much has to enter into the conversation somewhere along the way. No one likes to talk about death— not with family, not with strangers. It's just the kind of conversation that can really ruin a cocktail party. But when you're talking about life insurance, you're talking about money, not death. And money is okay, right? Money is our friend. Life insurance is about estate planning and the future and security. And money. Oh, and it's about investment, too. That's not so bad. And millions upon millions of Americans have life insurance. It sure seems silly to forego an investment opportunity or your loved ones' financial security just to avoid having an uncomfortable conversation.

A fourth reason people avoid jumping into the world of the happily life-insured is the process. No doubt, all those quotes and comparisons and different kinds of life insurance, all that proof of medical insurability and financial worth … it can all seem a little intimidating. We can help you with this in the next chapter as we take you on a little behind the scenes tour of how a life insurance company works and the things you will have to do when getting yourself that shiny, new policy.

3

A Look Behind the Curtain: What Happens When You Apply for Life Insurance

So maybe you don't have life insurance right now. Maybe you've cancelled your old coverage. Maybe you've just done a fine job over the years avoiding that pain in the neck life insurance salesman … even if he was your golf buddy for thirty years and your first cousin once removed. But you can't help but hear how things are changing in the life insurance market. You might've attended a seminar or two. Your friends have been talking. You're reading this book. You're beginning to think that life insurance might be a good investment after all. You're ready to leap onto this bandwagon, throw your hat in the ring, and apply for some. If you do, let us be the first to congratulate you on a good decision. Yes, we're insurance guys and so more than a little biased, but there are an awful lot of people out there who truly should have life insurance—to protect their families or for their own investment purposes—who don't.

Now that you've decided to take up this noble and profitable quest, we'd like to help you by running through the procedures, policy peculiarities, and possible pitfalls you will encounter as you navigate your way through the sometimes strange, always puzzling, but rarely exciting life insurance application process.

Buying Life Insurance: The Overview

Nowadays, the search for life insurance usually begins one of two places: at an insurance broker or at a computer. You either give the broker some information or you type it into the computer, and a bunch of price quotes from different insurance companies comes up based on a selection of different criteria. These criteria will include: where you live, your date of birth, height and weight, gender, a brief health history (possibly including questions about things like blood pressure and cholesterol), some lifestyle questions (have you been treated for alcoholism?, do you smoke?), some questions about family health history, and perhaps even some questions that seem more than a little irrelevant. They're not. Everything you provide is factored in. And depending on the criteria you give, insurance companies determine whether or not to offer you life insurance, what sort of insurance coverage to offer you, and what the price for that coverage will be.

If and when you do receive offers, the premiums you would have to pay could be more or less than someone else's, even if it is for the exact same level of coverage. Sometimes, the difference in premium payments can seem monstrous. This is because you have different qualifying criteria than that person. If you have heart disease and the other person doesn't, you'll pay a lot more for life insurance than that person because you're a greater health risk. If the other person is a professional lion trainer (and, really, is there any other kind?), that person will pay more than you because they have a much better chance of being eaten by an unhappy lion.

You see, insurance is a business, not a service. Insurance companies have every intention of turning a profit. You can't really blame them; just like you, they're pretty fond of money. In simplest terms, they make a profit by taking more money in from premiums than they have to pay out in benefits. To be more accurate, insurance companies usually take the money from premium payments and invest it, enabling that money to produce additional returns. So every time an insurance company approves an application for life insurance, it's betting that they will make more money from that policy's premiums and premium investment returns than they will have to pay to the beneficiaries if and when the benefit gets paid. If it looks like a bad bet—meaning it looks a lot like the company won't make a dime off the deal—the insurance company won't offer coverage. Additionally, the more likely it seems that an insurance company will have to pay out your benefit sooner rather than later, the more expensive your life insurance coverage is going to be. This improves the insurance company's chances of earning a profit off your policy. Investor-types will call this "speculation." The rest of us call this "gambling." And to the insurance industry, that's what offering insurance coverage is, basically. A big, fat gamble.

So where did all of these numbers come from? Who determined that a 63-year-old non-smoking male living in Connecticut but with a family history of heart disease pays such and such an annual premium for a life insurance policy worth $5 million?

Underwriting: What the Heck Is It?

Coming up with all of the numbers insurance companies use was hardly an overnight process. In some ways, this practice of risk assessment is as old as insurance itself. Older, even. Because in the old days, insurance wasn't called insurance; it was called *underwriting*. If someone back in 17ᵗʰ century England had wanted what we would now call life insurance, he would have gone to an underwriter, a private and wealthy individual who might offer to provide some sort of coverage based on a cursory exam. Generally, this exam pretty much consisted of the prospective client sticking out his tongue. Glands aren't swollen? Skin color okay? He seems chipper enough. Looks like the sort of fellow who might live another … oh, I dunno … shall we say, fifteen years? Good enough. Here's the policy I'll offer you. Here's what it'll cost. Do we have a deal?

To this day, this assessment analysis of cost versus risk is still called the *underwriting process*, and it's a big part of what happens every time a quote is requested or an application for insurance rolls into an insurance company.

The underwriting process gradually became more scientific in nature as underwriters began to get the feeling that looking at glands just might not be quite enough. In 1693, Dr. Edmund Halley—yep, the guy after whom the comet was named—produced the first modern *mortality table* (also called a *life table* or an *actuarial table*). This is a cheery statistical tool which shows what the probability is that a person of a given age will die before their next birthday. It was a lot less sexy than comet-watching, but it did give rise to a whole new statistical approach to insurance underwriting. By the end of the 17ᵗʰ century, statistical analysis and number-crunching were fast becoming a standard part of the underwriting process.

Things are far more sophisticated now. Information supplied by the applicant is run through a complex system of numerical and statistical comparisons. These comparisons are set up by mysterious figures called *actuaries*. Have you ever seen the Wizard of Oz? Remember the wizard? There was this big, mean talking head in a spooky, green castle that ruled over all of Oz with a thunderous voice. But when our heroes got into his throne room, they pull aside a curtain and find that the big head is really just an illusion produced by a little, weird, accountant-looking chap in striped pants who is sitting by some machine pulling levers and pushing buttons. He's the real wizard, the actual ruler of Oz. Look at that giant head as the insurance company. Actuaries are that odd fellow in striped pants. They are essentially professional mathematicians who sit at a computer all day pushing buttons, clicking their mouse, and analyzing numbers. The statistical information they produce is the basis for every single one of the insurance company's underwriting rules and premium rates. They rule Oz, but in a quiet, behind-the-curtain sort of way. We like to think that the word "actuary" comes from the fact that these are the guys who "actually" control the insurance industry. It's not true, but it should be. And I should know about actuaries. My paternal grandfather was the top actuary at a major life insurance company. As a seven year old, a trip to grandpa's house always included math problems for me to solve … for fun.

Most of the analytical heavy-lifting performed by actuaries over the years has been compiled in actuarial computer software. This software is capable of factoring in an enormous number of variables when making its calculations. So in today's digital age, when you or your broker puts in a request for a life insurance quote, this software chugs away for a second or two and in that second or two accesses many decades of mortality tables and statistics and other numerical tomfoolery to decide whether or not you are a good candidate for insurance, the amount and type of policies that would be best to offer you, and the cost of premium payments.

During this process, insurance companies generally simplify the classification of applicants by putting them into one of three risk groups: *preferred, standard*, or *substandard*. These are sometimes broken down further. *Preferred plus*, for instance, is the sort of classification Superman might get, since he pretty much can't die and so represents very little risk to the insurance company. Obviously, the lucky preferred folks get better premium rates than those classified as standard.

How Your Life Insurance Application Is Underwritten

Okay, so now let's say you've got your quote. It's looking good. You seem like a viable candidate, and the premium rates look pretty reasonable. Now, you have to fill out an official application. This asks many questions similar to those you answered when you got that quote but are usually more detailed. When you return this application, the underwriting process kicks in again.

In the case of an official life insurance application, the entire underwriting process is further broken down into medical and financial underwriting. Medical underwriting begins with your doctor and hospital records, including hospital chart notes, laboratory results or anything else that might be pertinent. An insurance company can't, however, go digging around these things unless you provide your explicit approval. A doctor's medical exam is usually also required, especially for high-value policies. This is the part people hate. Going to the doctor is never going to be as pleasant as that trip to Rome, but obviously insurance companies want to know everything there is to know about you, so there's just no getting around it. Often, your records and exam data are assessed together by your doctor, with the results summarized in an *Attending Physician Statement (APS)*. This APS gets shot off to the insurance company, where it is used as the primary tool for medical underwriting.

In contrast, financial underwriting is usually conducted from the applicant's own statements of income and net worth. Only in the case of high-value policies will the insurance company typically require secondary proof of income or net worth. Financial underwriting is primarily based on each individual insurance company's principles of what is called *insurance capacity*. Based on your net worth and income figures plus the company's own actuarial data, insurance companies will determine what your maximum allowable life insurance policy value will be. Quite often, this is a one-to-one ratio. That is, if you're worth $2 million, you can get yourself a life insurance policy worth a maximum of $2 million. Other insurance companies practice the "80% rule," where your insurance capacity is set at 80% of your total net worth. Under this rule, a person worth $2 million could get a policy valued at $1.6 million.

Sometimes, however, a company may be aggressively pursuing your business and will set your capacity at more than your net worth. This is a rare moment of desperate generosity for which insurance companies are not normally known. More commonly, a company's actuarial data indicate that it is wiser to be conservative and set an applicant's insurance capacity at considerably less than their total net worth. This is particularly true for applicants of advanced age for whom a sliding scale may be employed. The older the applicant, the smaller the insurance capacity because of the increased likelihood of imminent payout. It may seem cold-blooded, but those insurance companies want to make money on every transaction. If you're older, they might insure you, but the value of the policy will be less and the premium cost will be higher. Like Michael Corleone said in *The Godfather*, "It's not personal … it's strictly business."

Furthermore, someone of high net worth who is interested in a very high-value policy may find that he or she can't get that one-to-one insurance capacity ratio either. This is also a matter of simple economics. If someone worth a billion dollars buys a billion-dollar policy, paying out the benefit to that policy might just cripple an insurance company. Policies this valuable, therefore, are also subjected to a sliding scale, such that our billion-dollar policyholder might have their insurance capacity set at something more like $100 million or even less. So, take that, Mr. or Ms. Billionaire!

Term vs. Perm: The Classic Confrontation

Life is a complex spectacle, a sinuous dance of colors and light, a boiling cauldron of possibility full to overflowing with the chaos of consequences and a thousand million choices …

So is life insurance.

Except that in the sinuous dance of life insurance you don't really have a thousand million choices. That's a lot. But you do have quite a few when you apply for life insurance coverage, and they can get a bit mystifying unless you know exactly what those choices mean and how each choice will impact the terms of your policy and its value as an investment vehicle.

You might recall that we described term life insurance as insurance with an expiration date. These term policies are like snowflakes; they come in many shapes and sizes—one-year terms, two-year terms, 5-year terms, 10-year, 20-year, even 30-year terms are possible. Other term policies are set to run to a specific age, like to age 65 or 70. Basically, term insurance is as flexible as a Romanian gymnast. It's also very cheap for younger people. Since most traditional reasons why people purchase life insurance tend to be temporary conditions that will eventually go away, i.e. the kids grow up or the estate gains the value necessary to handle death costs, term insurance is often ideal.

But as an investment, it's usually a skunk in a sewer ... it stinks.

While we'll eventually delve into the details of life insurance investment, suffice it to say for now that a policy is only valuable from an investor's standpoint when the death benefit pays out. How often does a term policy pay out that death benefit? Just slightly more often than never. But don't take our word for it. In the spring of 1993, Penn State conducted an extensive study involving over 20,000 term policies worth an aggregate of about four billion dollars. Know how many of those term policies actually resulted in death benefit payout? One percent. A whopping one out of a hundred. This is because insurance companies count on the fact that most people who buy a term policy are going to survive the duration of that term. If the odds that someone will live to the end of the term are poor, the insurance company simply won't sell that person the insurance. For this reason, insurance companies will almost never sell term insurance for a term that ends past the applicant's 80th birthday. In fact, it starts becoming very difficult to obtain a term policy even at the relatively tender age of 65.

Now, that's not to say that no term policies are ever worth anything. If you are over 70 (or are younger but have a low life expectancy) and you still happen to have an active term policy, it just might fetch some interest on the market, especially if it's a high-value policy and your remaining life expectancy falls within the time left in the term. But generally even those with an active term policy will find that their best investment bet is to convert from term to permanent insurance, an option which we will discuss in more detail later in the book.

If you happen to be over 65 and don't yet have life insurance, don't fret. There are still options for your estate, your family, and for you to invest in your life. However, the process does become just a little more complex. Although companies will not offer you term insurance (in most cases), who cares? You don't want it anyway, because, as a rule, permanent insurance really is the way to go if you are entertaining notions of selling your policy.

The Pleasures of Permanence

Permanent insurance is exactly what its name suggests it is—it's permanent insurance. When you sign up for a permanent policy, you will never have to renew your life insurance coverage and never again have to worry about proving your insurability. The insurance company can't refuse to renew your term just because you actually had the gall to get older (how dare you) or because you contracted some health problem. You're a lifelong member of the club. No more hassles. No fuss, no bother. Forever and ever. Amen. In today's world of ever-increasing life expectancy, it's comforting to know that the only way you will ever be without life insurance is if you decide you want to be without life insurance.

And being hassle-free isn't permanent insurance's only advantage. If and when you decide to sell your policy, that permanent policy will look a whole lot sweeter to an investor than a term policy. If your policy were a used car, it's the difference between a mint condition Rolls Royce and a beat up Chevette with an oil leak.

Permanent policies also don't usually see the explosive premium increases that accompany term coverage renewals. On the contrary, the premium rates in many permanent policies are *level*, meaning they never increase. When you get toward 60 years old and term policy premium costs skyrocket, you will be paying the same premiums in these permanent policies as you paid when you were a young whippersnapper. Of course, up until that age, term policies are significantly cheaper. That's no big surprise. As the Penn State study pointed out, term policies hardly ever pay out, so insurance companies can afford to keep the premiums low and still turn a nice, plump profit.

But there are two other reasons why permanent policy premiums cost so much. The first one, to be brutally frank, is greed. Insurance salesmen and brokers often get a much bigger commission when they sell a permanent policy versus term coverage. This and any other administrative fees are collectively and appropriately called the policy's *load*, probably because it hangs like a millstone around your policy's neck, weighing it down with hidden charges.

The second reason is because the policy owner is usually paying into the policy's *cash value*.

Cash Value and the Sin of Surrender

Cash value is a savings account associated with a permanent life insurance policy. That's about it. You may see or hear other more complicated descriptions. Ignore them. Cash value is a savings account. The end.

Each time you pay a premium for a permanent insurance policy, a portion of the money usually goes into that policy's cash value monetary reserve. This stored up cash is normally used to keep your premiums from increasing as you get older when your cost of insurance would otherwise increase drastically. How the cash value accomplishes this varies a bit depending on which type of permanent insurance policy you have, but the principle is always the same: cash value is accumulated money held in reserve to be utilized to keep your future premium costs down.

So now you have this money stored in a reserve ... waiting. But you don't want to see your money sitting around doing nothing. It's not earning interest. It's not working for a living. It spends the whole day watching soap operas and drinking schnapps. No one likes lazy money. So the insurance company takes the money in the cash value reserve and invests it. This way, that money gains additional value in more or less the same manner as money in a savings account earns interest.

Now, that cash value money hasn't been locked away in some deep, secret vault where you can never get at it. It is, after all, your money. The insurance company is just sort of hanging onto it for you, investing it, keeping it safe and warm and snug. If at some point you decide to willingly cancel, or *surrender*, your permanent life policy, you will get back all the cash value, including any interest it has earned, but minus the policy's surrender charges. Any cash value (minus charges) will also be returned if you just stop paying your policy premiums. The surrender charges, however, can be shockingly steep. Insurance companies like to think of this as their caretaker wages for all those long years of feeding and watering your money. Fortunately, surrender charges are often waived if the canceled policy has been in force for a long time. The net amount of the cash value you will get back when you surrender your policy after the surrender charges have been taken out is called the policy's *surrender value*.

The surrender value has always been viewed as a permanent policy's safety net should you absolutely need quick cash or want to get rid of the policy for any reason. But policy surrender is also a market transaction; you're reselling a "used" policy just like you might sell your used car. Imagine, however, a situation where the only person to whom you could sell your car is the dealer from which you bought it. There would be no market pressure, and you'd get virtually nothing for it when you did want to sell it. This is the exact situation folks with life insurance have faced when they wanted to surrender their policies. The only "price" they could get in return for "selling" their policy back to the insurance company was the return of the money and interest in the cash value reserve, minus the possibly exorbitant surrender charges. Too often, these surrender charges devoured all the profit that money made in interest and then some. So the insurance company often makes out quite well in these situations. The consumer ... not so much.

But now there is another safety net option out there. Thanks to new market pressures, a policy seller no longer has to settle for a whole lot of nothing much. There is considerably more to gain than just the return of your own money—minus those surrender charges, of course. Nowadays, selling a used policy doesn't just mean a safety net—it means net profit.

Permanent Insurance Comes in Many Tasty Flavors

There are three major variants of permanent life insurance, with countless mutant variations and hybrids thrown into the mix to keep things nice and confusing. These permanent insurance variants primarily differ in one way: how the cash value is handled. From this one difference spring all the other differences, i.e. whether the death benefit is guaranteed or whether premium payments are fixed at a certain price.

<u>Whole Life</u>

Whole life, sometimes also called *ordinary life* or *straight life*, is the oldest form of permanent insurance. It's also the most secure or the most rigidly inflexible, depending on whether you're a glass-is-half-full or half-empty kind of person. Standard whole life works like this ... When you sign up for a whole life policy, you're basically signing up for annual term coverage that is renewed automatically each year until you turn 100 years old. Of course, as you get older that term coverage would get more expensive, its premium costs climbing each year until, eventually, they would hit the stratosphere and become unaffordable. Whole life attacks this nasty little problem through the use of the cash value reserve.

To put it simply, the money in the cash value reserve is included as part of the death benefit payout. If there's a $5 million policy with $1 million in cash value built up, the death benefit would consist of the $1 million in cash value plus $4 million out of the insurance company's pocket. The part of the death benefit that comes out of the insurance company's own coffers is called the *net amount at risk*.

When a whole life policy owner pays a premium, you can imagine that one part of the payment is designed to cover the current cost of insurance for the net amount at risk. This cost is called the *mortality charge*. The other part is a contribution to the cash value reserve. As the cash value builds, the net amount at risk for the insurance company goes down. This means that the mortality charge goes down as well, since the amount of insurance it is paying for is decreasing. But as a person ages, they increase as an insurance risk, so the cost of insuring them goes up. The cash value, then, is used to offset the escalating cost of insurance due to increased risk with the decreased cost due to the lowering of the net amount at risk. For all intents and purposes, a whole life policyholder is actually paying for and getting less "pure" insurance coverage with each premium paid, because the cash value grows and the insurance company has less at risk.

Whole life policies guarantee an annual fixed rate of return on any money stored in the cash value reserve. This rate is usually very conservative from an investment perspective, but it tends to be comparable to the standard interest rate you would expect from a bank savings account. When the insurance company invests your cash value but those investments don't do well, you are still assured of earning that fixed rate of return. This guarantees that the cash value will grow at a stable, predetermined pace, neither faster nor slower than initially planned.

To accommodate the inflexible nature of this structure, whole life policies can't offer you a lot of choices. The death benefit is guaranteed but can't be changed once the policy is in force. Premium payments are fixed and level. No flexibility there, either. But on the plus side, your cash value will never lose money; it will always grow at the same steady, secure, sleepy snail's pace.

Variable Life

Variable life is a variation of whole life that enables the insured to choose a more aggressive cash value investment path from the insurance company's portfolio of stocks, bonds and money-market funds. This makes a much larger rate of return possible. But as Uncle Ben says in the *Spiderman* movie, "With great power comes great responsibility." Whole life's fixed rate of return, while small, also provides protection. If the investments lose money, an insurance company is still obligated to beef your cash value up by that fixed rate of return. If you choose poor investments with a variable life policy, your cash value can lose worth. If things really go south, you could lose all your cash value. It's like doing an Irish jig on a tightrope. And if you lose that cash value reserve, you'll have nothing to help you manage those painfully high insurance cost increases when you get older, and that could leave you uninsured. Oops.

As in whole life, the cash value of a variable policy covers part of the death benefit payout. As the cash value builds, the net amount at risk goes down. As the amount at risk goes down, the mortality charges decrease, offsetting the increase to the mortality charge as the insured ages. Also like whole life, premium payments are fixed and level. But unlike whole life, the cash value itself is not guaranteed and can lose money. Rather than raise premium costs if the cash value investments do poorly, the death benefit is reduced instead. The result is that the death benefit can bounce up and down like a ping pong ball depending on how the cash value investment is doing. (Although some variable contracts do allow for a guaranteed minimum death benefit even if the cash value investment bombs.) If at any time the mortality charge for the net amount at risk is more than the fixed premium payment, the policy will terminate. This unfortunate turn of events generally only happens if the cash value investment has absolutely tanked.

Universal Life

In recent times, the Best in Show first-place blue ribbon of the permanent life insurance pageant usually goes to *universal life*. There are good reasons for this. First, it offers a lot of flexibility. Rather than offer a fixed interest rate on cash value, like whole life, or no return rate guarantees, like variable life, universal life splits the difference. It takes a less conservative investment path than whole life, enabling it to offer a better rate of return in most years. If the investments don't perform, however, the cash value rate of return bottoms out at a guaranteed minimum rate, so your money won't ever make less than that rate in any given year. This gives it security that variable life lacks.

Furthermore, universal life allows for periodic increases in the death benefit (with commensurate increases in premium payments). The death benefit in a universal policy is guaranteed; it won't go down like it can in a variable policy unless you request a reduction. But best of all, universal life offers flexibility in premium payments. How? By allowing you to vary how much you pay into your cash value account. Some industry people insist on calling the cash value reserve in a universal life policy an *accumulation fund*, instead. Ostensibly, they do this because the cash value in a universal policy behaves a bit differently than that in a whole life policy. We think this is silly. Life is too confusing already. So we're sticking with the term "cash value." No one in the world enjoys complicating simple things more than the insurance industry. Then we get to write books explaining it all.

In a whole life policy, the amount of money that goes into the cash value is rigidly controlled with each premium payment. Not so with a universal life policy. You can pay as much or as little into the cash value as you want. This obviously means that the premium payments are wildly flexible. As long as you pay enough with each premium payment to cover the mortality charge (and the policy's load), your policy will stay in force. Money can be taken from the cash value to help pay a premium's mortality charge, assuming, of course, that your cash value has enough to cover it. You can even miss entire premium payments as long as your cash value doesn't run out. You can build your cash value quickly or not at all. It's all up to you. It's a wealth of choices. Though it should be pointed out that not paying into a cash value account now will mean astronomically high premiums later when your mortality charge goes way up. That might mean you won't be able to afford your insurance, so beware!

Investors can't get enough universal life policies. They just love them. If universal life policies were chocolates, they'd eat themselves sick. If you want to win the heart of an insurance investor, tell them you'll sell them your universal life policy. Why? Because investors don't care one single, solitary fig for cash value; they only want to pay the mortality charge. The flexibility of universal life lets them do that. Now that's certainly not to say that other forms of permanent insurance won't float their boats. But if you really want to make investors salivate, universal life is the no-brainer, slam dunk choice.

Sign on the Dotted Line ...

So, you've survived the underwriting process. You've chosen what type of insurance you want and your coverage options. Your application looks just peachy. The insurance company likes your style. You passed the interview. You've got the stuff of champions. And they'd like you to join their team.

The insurance company will send you a contract. This contract consists of your application and the medical and financial data you supplied to the insurance company just in case you forgot who you are. It also consists of dozens—maybe even hundreds—of policy specifications and legal provisions. We shall now embark on a detailed and thorough discussion of each and every one of these provisions ... Ha. Just kidding. We're your friends. We would never subject you to a fate so horrible.

There is however, one important concept that you should be familiar with called *incontestability*. The incontestability clause states that the contract is null and void if the insured made a material misrepresentation on the application and dies during the first two years of coverage. In every single life insurance contract, it is specifically stated that if the policyholder is discovered to have lied on their application and it is deemed to be a *material misrepresentation*—a heart condition, a smoking habit, a problem on the driving record, a fudging of personal net worth, or any other representation that is deemed to be material—the insurance company has the option to *rescind*, or revoke, the contract without any warning within the first two years. After two years, it is assumed that the insurance company will have had the opportunity to discover any material misrepresentation, and the policy becomes "incontestable." At that stage, the insurance company must prove a *fraud* occurred for them to rescind a contract or deny a claim.

Now what's the difference between material misrepresentation and fraud, you might ask? Excellent question. We don't really know. Honestly. That's a question being answered differently in different cases by different lawyers in different parts of the country every day. But believe us, insurance companies have good lawyers. Really, really good lawyers. To avoid this sort of legal grief, there is one time-tested strategy that we highly recommend. As your mom used to say, "Just tell the truth, honey." It's that simple. We mention this only because some people really, really like to cheat on their net worth or are pushed to do so by unscrupulous promoters or insurance agents. Higher net worth equals more death benefit; more death benefit equals higher premiums and commissions. So what's an extra million or two, right? Well, don't do it. It's an exceptionally bad idea that can lead to no end of trouble. If you tell the insurance company the truth on their application, you have absolutely no reason to worry about your policy being rescinded or a claim not being paid.

So that's it. You read through your contract, sign it, send it back and … *voila!* … you've joined the happy crew of the S.S. Insured. That wasn't really so bad, was it? And ahh … nothing beats that fresh, new policy smell …

4

Lessons from the Past: The Problem with Old Life Insurance Investment Strategies

Okay, we're going to make some assumptions at this point. We're going to assume that you either have a life insurance policy now or that you know the process you need to go through to get one. We're also going to assume that you know what kind of policy to pick based on your needs. If none of this is true, it means you probably skipped Chapter 3. That's okay. No, really. It's fine. Though ... it does hurt a little. If you must know, we'll probably have a good cry later. When you're not looking.

Additionally, we're now going to assume that you have an understanding of the most basic terminology used in the life insurance business. If you're missing that ... well, that's Chapter 2. Please reread. There'll be a quiz later, and it will count toward your final grade ... We're only joshing, of course. Your final grade is based entirely on personality. And we like you.

See now, here's where we're going to start getting into the real business of this book. We just want to make sure that you've got a solid foundation on which to build your cathedral of investment opportunity. So if you're with us, if you're ready, let's fall in line and march boldly on ...

Cash Value as an Investment

Using a life insurance policy as an investment is hardly a new notion. Actually, it's very nearly as old as whole life insurance itself, since the principles upon which whole life were founded included the concept of cash value. It seemed like a good idea then and, frankly, still seems to make sense now. You've got this life insurance policy, this asset, that you need to have, and part of this asset is growing tax-deferred within the policy. Might as well make it work for you. So the insurance company invests that money for you. That makes more money. That's all good. So what's the problem? Whole and universal life policies do not present much of a problem at all. They have always been viewed as a fairly conservative investment with a tax-deferred growth within the insurance policy. In the days of the booming stock and real estate markets, these policies were criticized for their lower then "market" rates of return. However, in the recent economic turmoil, these policies have proved to be very stable, especially whole life policies. But what about variable and variable universal life policies? Weren't they designed to keep your cash value's head above inflation's treacherous waters? Sure, but those boats have holes, too.

While people in the insurance industry certainly do enjoy the brokering fees they collect for managing your variable policy's investments, that aggressive investment stuff really isn't their style. Insurance folks generally aren't in love with the high risk associated with securities-based investments, which is why they don't guarantee investment returns for a variable policy. Don't go crying to them if the stock market tanks and all that money you've been socking away in your policy's cash value suddenly disappears in a puff of black smoke. You chose your aggressive investment package and you assumed the risk.

But the insurance company really doesn't want you to lose your cash value. Sweet of them, isn't it? Bet you never even knew how much they cared. Of course, they're really just afraid that when your cash value shrinks, you won't have enough money in reserve to keep your premium costs down as time goes by. This just might cause you to let your policy lapse because you no longer want to pay those escalating premium costs. If this happens when you're much older, they'll be happy to see you go. That just means they get to avoid paying your death benefit. But if you fly away too early, they miss out on all those years of premium payments. And that makes them very sad. But not being able to afford your life insurance because you blew away all your cash value will make you sad, too. And now, everyone is sad.

Lots of people got burned by this in the early 90's, when variable policies were all the rage. Low- to mid-level insurance agents were selling them in droves and putting their clients' cash value into mutual funds. And why not? The stock market was booming; any securities-based investment seemed like a can't-miss proposition. When the inevitable happened and the bubble burst, stocks took a nosedive and so did the cash value of those variable policies. Policyholders folded up the tents, surrendered their policies to take whatever little money was left in them, and ran to the hills never to be seen again.

Here's the funny thing ... Even if you assume that risk, "damn the torpedoes", and go with a variable policy, you're still unlikely to get the sort of return you would've gotten had you just invested that money through usual investment channels. It goes back to what we mentioned earlier—insurance companies aren't investment brokers or banks. What they do best is sell insurance. That's not to say that they're *bad* at investing. But investment firms and banks tend to do it a little better. Look at it this way … do you order lasagna at a steak house? Do you go to a Chinese restaurant for a blueberry blintz? It's not much different than letting an insurance company do your investing for you.

Some life insurance companies tried to overcome this hurdle by hiring investment companies to manage the funds within their variable life policies. Good idea? It seemed so, but the investment companies had to make a profit, too. Guess who wound up paying those extra commissions in the form of additional fees and charges? You got it … the policyholder. And so there went a sizeable piece of the increased rate of return, which was the whole reason the policyholder had assumed the risk of a variable policy in the first place.

What policyholders hungry for investment profit often forget is that the real purpose of cash value isn't so much to make you gobs of money as it is to keep your life insurance affordable when you get older. This job, it performs admirably well; in fact, many industry people will argue that it's the only thing the cash value in a life insurance policy is good for. These same folks would suggest that properly investing the money that ordinarily goes into a cash value reserve elsewhere will generate much higher returns and therefore enable the insured to pay those much higher premiums when they age anyway. This is usually true, but not everyone has the discipline to do it. The *forced savings* element of a cash value policy can be an attractive characteristic to those slightly less disciplined among us who would be more inclined to buy a waterproof high definition television for the shower rather than invest.

And cash value does have some other benefits as well. The more conservative forms of cash value investment can be useful for diversifying an investment portfolio by offsetting more aggressive investments made elsewhere. Also, you can borrow against your cash value money as if you were taking out a loan from a bank. If you borrow money like this, you will usually be assessed fees, but the good news is that there is no credit review or official application, which can be practical for some. Also, while cash value money is not FDIC-insured, it is often protected by the life and health guaranty funds that most states have. This is a safeguard that most other investment vehicles don't offer. Plus, the guaranty limits of this state-based protection are actually often considerably higher than that offered by the FDIC, so it's nice to know you are usually well-protected in the admittedly unlikely event that your insurance company goes insolvent.

Perhaps cash value's best—and most interesting—asset is the fact that it grows tax deferred. Even the dividends paid out from cash value investment are usually not taxable. As a result, more than one scheme has been cooked up using a life insurance policy's cash value as a tax shelter. This is particularly useful for wealthy estates which have tended to use cash value reserves and their tax-deferred status as valuable estate planning tools.

In spite of these qualities, cash value has rather deservedly earned itself a reputation as being a weak investment vehicle. Over the last several decades, an industry mantra emerged: "Buy term and invest the rest." This gradually became the predominant philosophy of an entire segment of industry professionals who, is some circles, have become known as "termites." The termites go by the belief that *all* life insurance needs are temporary, that there in no such thing as a permanent need for life insurance coverage. They only recommend term insurance and wouldn't touch a permanent policy unless they were dressed in a protective chemical suit. They say to forget about that forced savings stuff, go spontaneously generate that discipline you might never have had, eschew that high def TV in the shower and invest that money elsewhere.

Fair enough. But there are two gargantuan problems with this mentality. First, is it an ironclad truth that investing all that money as you go along will eliminate any need for life insurance coverage later in life? Of course not. The termites simply assume that no older person will ever want life insurance, which, to be honest, is ridiculous. Boiling it all down, life insurance is really about two things: estate management and disaster protection. Neither of these needs disappears when you get older. Sure, estates gain value, but factoring life insurance in as an element in any estate planning can help minimize the difficulties surviving loved ones face and maximize the value of the estate for them. And what happens if investments don't pan out or if a fearsome economic downtick or a vicious stock market plunge gobbles up most of your money? What if there is a family catastrophe? It's a nice thing to know that no matter what happens your loved ones will be secure because you have a life insurance policy in your back pocket.

Secondly—and this really is a big one—termites are mired scalp-deep in jurassically old traditional thinking. As much as they paint themselves as revolutionaries, as much as they might see themselves as bravely fighting for the client, they're missing the boat on what is really happening in the life insurance industry today. They have tirelessly spread the gospel that permanent insurance is a bad investment. They're wrong. Devastatingly wrong, in fact. Their endlessly repeated message has deafened them to the rumblings of a changing marketplace. What termites should be preaching is that cash value is a bad investment. The great majority of us in the life insurance industry already agree with that assessment. The new way of thinking isn't that the value of a permanent life insurance policy is in the cash value; it's in the policy itself. On one hand, that policy pays out a large, tax-free benefit if it is held until the death of the policyholder. On the other hand, that policy is a solid asset, not because it can generate some paltry interest return, but because if you choose to hold it until your death, your family or beneficiary will enjoy significant benefits and if you choose to sell it *a lot of people will pay you a lot of money for it.*

That's the real revolution.

That's why we wrote this book.

And So It Begins: The Roots of the Secondary Life Insurance Market

Ahh, the 80's. Remember them? Those were interesting times. The rise of computers. The fall of the Communist Bloc. The explosion of cable television. Michael Jackson hadn't yet turned his face into a science experiment. Ronald Reagan was president. E.T phoned home. Johnny Carson still ruled late night TV. A strong dollar. Cell phones …

AIDS.

It rose quietly, like a specter, spreading its arms until its cold fingers touched an entire decade. People were afraid of water fountains, of toilet seats. They wouldn't shake hands anymore. And when its fingers found the throat of the life insurance industry, they very nearly throttled it to death.

AIDS was killing a lot of people. Young people, most of them. A lot of them were people who had always been healthy. Many of these people had life insurance policies, possibly even preferred status policies because many had been so young and healthy. In the earliest days of the disease, it was even possible to take out policies after diagnosis because so little was understood about it. And insurance companies were getting pummeled. Not only were they paying out huge numbers of death benefits, they were also losing a lot of younger policyholders from whom they were counting on long years of premium payments. It was a devastating one-two punch that nearly knocked the reeling life insurance industry down for the count. The industry needed to do something—and fast.

So it did.

It created *accelerated death benefits (ADBs).*

The concept is a simple one. Insurance companies approached policyholders who had been diagnosed with a terminal condition like AIDS and made them an offer: Rather than waiting for the insured person to die and then have to pay out the full face amount of the policy's death benefit to the beneficiaries, insurance companies offered to pay a smaller portion of the benefit directly to the policyholder while he or she was still alive. The amount they offered might be 40% of the death benefit. Maybe 50%, 60%, even 70%. The important thing was that the insurance company drastically reduced its liability.

Let's take a hypothetical case. Let's say it is 1985, and there is a 35-year-old male named Ray who is diagnosed with AIDS. Based on the knowledge of the disease at that time, Ray's prognosis is that his remaining life expectancy is less than two years. He has a $1 million life insurance policy. His insurance company then approaches him with an accelerated death benefit offer of, say, $600,000. He now has a choice. He could take that $600,000 for himself now, or he could refuse the offer and let his beneficiaries receive the full $1 million benefit after he passes on. Obviously, the insurance company really, really wants him to take that $600,000. Based on the life expectancy, the insurance company is pretty darn certain that they're going to have to pay out something within the next two years or so. They'd much rather it be $600,000 than $1 million.

Many stricken policyholders accepted these offers. True, policyholders who had built up cash value in their policies could surrender that policy to get their cash reserve back (with all of the surrender charges taken out, of course), but the amount of money paid out in an ADB was significantly more. The quality of life for a lot of policyholders was much improved by that money. Many no longer had to worry about income, taking away one terrible burden that could otherwise shadow them at the end of their days. Others could turn that money right around and use it for treatments and drugs that weren't covered by insurance and that they wouldn't otherwise have been able to afford. Still others were entirely without health insurance of any kind, and the ADB proved to be the one and only way they could hope to receive any sort of treatment. Yes, the beneficiaries lost out, but accelerated death benefits seemed like a fair way to enable a terminally ill person, especially a younger one, to cope with their condition. They really helped a lot of people put as happy an ending as possible to what was ultimately still a painful and tragic story.

Oh, yeah … And insurance companies saved money.

In fact, they saved a fortune.

Why Your Life Insurance Policy Is Worth Something: The Creation of the Secondary Life Insurance Market

The 80's were known for one more thing—money. It was the "me decade." The slogan for the entire decade would eventually come straight from the Gordon Gekko character in the movie *Wall Street*: "Greed is good." Money was back in style in a big way, and everyone was scheming up new tricks to make more of it.

When interest rates went flatter than a hammered pancake, some investors got itchy. Where could they make up the shortfall? What else could they invest in? Where, in heaven's name, could they make more money?

Then they saw what the life insurance industry was doing. They saw accelerated death benefits at work.

They had an idea.

What if they could buy out a life insurance policy on a terminally ill patient before the insurance company got to it. If they owned the policy, then they could collect the whole death benefit when the insured person passed away. A terminally ill patient with pressing monetary needs didn't care a lick whether he or she sold their life insurance policy to the insurance company or to an investor, just as long as there was a nice chunk of ready cash in it for them.

Of course, once a sale was made not every terminally ill patient wound up passing away before the next premium payment was due. Once the original policyholder had sold their policy to an investor, they certainly weren't going to pay the premiums on that policy anymore. In order for the policy to stay in force, someone had to pay the premiums, so the investors, as the new policy owners, started paying the premiums themselves.

And so it was that a maverick group of eager and aggressive investors set out to buy life insurance policies. Often, they could beat the life insurance company to a potential sale and reap the profits uncontested. Other times, a bidding war between the insurance company and an investor would ensue. But the insurance companies, slaves to bureaucratic overhead and actuarial data that they are, could rarely compete in bidding wars with aggressive and sometimes downright reckless investors. Furthermore, once an investor got the ball rolling and had their first few death benefit payouts, they would be **swimming** in ready cash. They could turn that money right around and plow it straight back into buying more policies. Insurance companies didn't always have this kind of cash available. They had to be careful to conserve enough money to ensure that they could pay out all the claims they were being bombarded with. The result was that more and more of these third-party investor deals were transacted, so much so, in fact, that they got their own name: *viatical settlements*.

Just to be clinical about this, the technical definition of a viatical is a transaction where the life insurance policy of a person with a low life expectancy is purchased by a third-party investor for investment purposes. The life expectancy of the insured generally must be no longer than two or (rarely) three years, meaning that the insured has almost always been diagnosed with a terminal illness or condition. For the duration of the policy, the investor is responsible for all premium payments to keep the policy in force. And that's it in a Webster's Dictionary sort of nutshell.

In the American life insurance industry, viatical settlements were a revelation, a terror, an absolute conundrum. The industry didn't know what to make of this new development. A *secondary market* of life insurance investors? It was as if the sun started rising in the west.

Only one thing was absolutely certain …

The winds of change were blowing like a hurricane.

5

Taming the Wild West: The Secondary Life Insurance Market Today

Have you, by any chance, ever read anything about the Old West? Interesting times in our country's history. In those days, a young, eager United States was still pushing its western border past the Mississippi and across the plains, striving for the distant Pacific coast and stretching out toward the sunset.

First went the explorers, daring souls keen to experience something that no one like them had ever known before. They learned the rules of survival in that strange and hostile place, then passed them on, serving as guides and frontiersmen to the next wave of stout, resolute types who followed them to the wild lands. These were the settlers, stalwart pioneers who gambled their lives, their homes, their families, and everything they had on the golden opportunities this untamed land offered. So far, so good. But when those settlers began to plant roots, another group wandered its way westward.

Profiteers.

These were unscrupulous characters, snake oil salesmen quick to find angles to exploit while living among people struggling to make sense of their new world. The profiteers dreamed up all sorts of tricks and scams, all manner of ways to take advantage of a place where laws did not exist or could not be enforced. They were dangerous people, slippery and downright mean. They wore black hats. They twiddled pencil-thin mustaches. They laughed sinister, villainous laughs while they got rich off sinister, villainous schemes. It would take some time before law enforcement and the legal infrastructure would mature enough to catch up with these types. But when the fist of justice finally did come down, it came down hard, and the swindlers either cleared out of town or were left swinging from the scaffolds ...

This is about when we imagine you're wondering what the heck any of this has to do with life insurance. The short answer is ... well ... a whole lot, actually. In fact, in terms of the newly emergent secondary life insurance market of the 1980's, it's almost exactly the same story ...

31

Growing Pains: Problems with the Early Secondary Life Insurance Market

Those first investment mavericks who beat the banks to viatical settlements probably never realized just how huge a market those transactions would ultimately create. But by the time the 80's drew to a close, those visionary frontiersmen had shown the way for bigger fish, and a secondary market for life insurance was no longer such a rogue concept. More investors were surging to this new market; more life insurance policies were being sold to those investors. In 1989, a small handful of investment firms began buying viaticals on an exclusive basis, and so the American secondary life insurance market created its first dedicated, full-time, button-down professionals in the form of viatical settlement companies, often called *viatical providers*. The market was gaining momentum; this new territory was becoming settled. And with that momentum came fresh, sparkling streams of cash. There was gold in them thar' hills.

But as the market for viatical settlements grew by leaps and bounds in the early 1990's, it began drawing the wrong kind of attention. Black hat-wearing, mustache-twiddling profiteers saw virgin ground that was rich and fertile, new land where money-making scams, investment cons and Ponzi schemes could bear fruit and thrive. They came to this new market in flocks because there was no regulation yet, no real laws governing viatical settlements, no established industry track-record or standards. There was no sheriff in this town.

So fraud swept through the newborn industry like a brushfire, threatening to burn down the barn before it was even built. By the time the mid-90's rolled around, some have estimated that as many as one out of every four viatical settlement deals was actually a scam.

And viatical scams were like a box of crayons ... they came in a colorful assortment. Sometimes, it was the insured person, known in viatical transactions as the *viator*, who was duped. More commonly, however, fraud was committed on viatical investors. In a number of the more audacious cases, fast-talking exploitation experts masquerading as viatical providers even sold policies for viators who didn't exist, and life insurance companies, curmudgeons that they are, aren't especially keen on paying death benefits out for fake policies issued on fictional people.

But while there once was a time when you could have shot a man stone dead in the streets of Deadwood because he smelled funny, you would be ill-advised to try that today. Similarly, while there once was a time where swindlers and shysters held sway over viaticals, the law eventually found its way into the secondary life insurance market with the purposeful swagger of a deputized gunfighter. Many of the unsavory practices that were widespread in the 80's and early- to mid-90's were dragged out into the light of day, publicly identified and largely stamped out by regulation and legislation. In 1993, the National Association of Insurance Commissioners (NAIC) was formed to develop industry regulations and licensing requirements. In that same year, NAIC released the first edition of the *Model Viatical Settlement Act*, sometimes shortened to the *Model Act*, which was designed to regulate the sale of insurance policies by people with a terminal illness or condition. This act would eventually become the basis for the secondary life insurance market laws that have so far been put into force in 35 U.S. states as of this writing.

It should be pointed out, however, that just because legislation and law enforcement appeared on the scene doesn't mean that everything in the land of viatical settlements was roses and sugarplums. While it certainly cleaned out most of the filth, some fraud and corruption in the secondary life insurance market still exists. Now, however, a selection of laws and regulations are in place in most states to deal with this sort of malfeasance. Nevertheless, you still need to be careful when dealing with the secondary market and should always work through reputable providers and individuals with a proven track record of success in the industry. (We'll be talking a lot more about working with the secondary market later in this book. We just figure it's never too early to drop a warning on you.)

Not all the trouble with viaticals stemmed from fraud, though. Many problems arose from the fact that most investors had precious little experience handling life insurance policies. The procedures, the concepts, the whims and vagaries of the industry left them lost in the weeds. Like, for instance, when mistakes were made while assessing a potential viator's life expectancy. In these cases, investors got stuck watching the return on their investment plummet steadily as they shoveled out more money for premium after premium to keep the viator's policy in force. In extreme cases, the investor could see the entirety of their investment whittled away as their viator just kept hanging around, stubbornly refusing to pass on.

At no time was this effect more apparent than in 1996. This was about the time when the protease inhibitor was developed and put into widespread use for those diagnosed with AIDS. Prior to the protease inhibitor and the antiretroviral drug cocktails, a person diagnosed with full-blown AIDS would be expected to pass away within nine months. On average, the protease inhibitor added about eight years to an AIDS patient's life expectancy, with some patients living twelve years longer or more. This was spectacular news to a world ravaged by a horrific affliction. It was less spectacular for viatical investors holding the life insurance policies of those AIDS patients. And since the policies of AIDS patients still comprised the largest part of the viatical market, the advent of the protease inhibitor set the whole business on its ear.

The upshot of this episode was so traumatic to the industry that it earned its own name: the *miracle cure effect*.

As if fraud, investor inexperience and the miracle cure effect weren't enough for the newborn secondary life insurance market to wrestle with, the very insurance industry itself took steps to crush it. It's not surprising. The reason insurance companies came up with accelerated death benefits was so that they would be able to cut their losses from the AIDS epidemic. Yet every policy bought for a viatical settlement was one that would have to be paid the full death benefit. Insurance companies wanted to pay the reduced accelerated benefit, instead. So it became a race, and insurance companies, grown chubby on many decades of accumulated bureaucracy, weren't very fast movers. It took a while for insurance companies to catch their breath and get on the offensive.

When they did, though, they struck a good, solid blow. They improved their accelerated death benefit payouts to make themselves more competitive with viatical rates. They also made accelerated benefits much more widely available, and many began offering them as an additional optional rider for life insurance policies. It meant that policyholders now knew about the accelerated benefits offered by the insurance companies before they had ever even heard about viatical settlements. Mobility was no longer an issue. Plus, many companies even charged extra for the accelerated benefit rider, making it a little profit-maker besides.

While these industry moves didn't exactly kill the viatical business—it proved a resilient beast—they did go some long way toward curbing its exponential growth.

And yet, against all conceivable odds—despite the rampant fraud, the investor blunders, the insurance industry's near-militant resistance—the viatical industry kept chugging away. How it managed to survive, even grow, in spite of all these obstacles is nothing less than a modern-day wonder. It is, in the end, a testament to the strength of the concepts underlying the secondary market for life insurance. Despite the barriers and countless errors in execution, it was too good an idea to die. So the market just kept getting bigger and bigger and bigger …

And that's when it hit a real problem. An implacable, unyielding, unconquerable, undeniable, impossible brick wall of a problem.

The market ran out of policies to buy.

Now, that's not to say that more potential policies weren't being generated. As we all unfortunately know, people are being diagnosed with life-threatening conditions every day. Some of those people have life insurance policies. Each of those was a potential viator. But the market had grown to the point where there simply weren't enough new potential viators to meet the appetite of investors. And with protease inhibitors having more or less eliminated the AIDS-driven viator market, investors, it seemed, had drunk the money river dry. Sure, they could keep putting out the call for new viators, signing them up as they became available. But the market had exhausted its ability to expand. Like the Wild West more than a century and a half earlier, its border had reached the ocean. The Wild West was tamed and fully settled now. No room for latecomers. The gravy train was tapped out. All the gold had been mined from the hills and panned from the rivers. Time to move on ... right?

Oh, not so fast ...

Life Settlements Take the Stage

The principles behind the secondary life insurance market were sound. As a market, it was maturing, and it was gradually becoming more institutionalized by the increasing presence of companies with long histories in the investment business and established investment practices. Many of the conmen had been drummed out of town by new legislation and enforcement. The future of the secondary life insurance market should have been as rosy as the sunrise. If only investors could find more policies to buy ...

Then ...

They did.

It suddenly dawned on the investment community that a policy they bought didn't necessarily have to belong to someone already diagnosed with a terminal condition. As long as the investor was willing to foot the bill for the premiums, an insured person could have a life expectancy of three years, four years, five, even ten years or more. If the investor accounted for the uncertainty, if the price for the policy was conservatively set so that the investor could still expect to turn a profit even if the insured lived eight or ten years or more, then what did it matter? As long as investors planned for the longer life expectancy of the insured, there was no reason why they couldn't apply the same principles of a viatical transaction: buy the policy, pay the premiums to keep it in force, collect the death benefit. What was the difference?

Clearly, there's a little more risk to the investor in this sort of longer term arrangement. Looking at it from an investment angle, the longer the insured lives, the lower the investment rate of return because the investor has to keep feeding money into the investment in the form of premium payments. An investor could even lose money if the sum paid to the insured to purchase the policy plus the premiums paid to keep the policy in force equaled more than the death benefit. As a result, a policy belonging to someone with a shorter life expectancy was still most desirable. So who had shorter life expectancies without having been diagnosed with a fatal illness or condition? Older life insurance policyholders. The older, frankly, the better, since it meant less risk that the policyholder would live a long time past the projected life expectancy.

In fact, many older policyholders had seen their need for life insurance diminish over the years and so might have otherwise surrendered their policy, anyway. The only thing they would've gotten out of that is the return of the cash value—minus any surrender charges—and the fact that they wouldn't have to pay premiums anymore. That's all fine, but not exactly grounds for throwing a party. Instead, they could sell that unwanted policy to investors for a rich payoff during those retirement years, which, of course, tends to be exactly when income dries up. That payoff was usually worth far, far more than the cash value a policy had stored up in it. It was almost like someone offering you a small fortune for a ratty old recliner you sort of want to throw out anyway. And that *was* worth a party. A big one with pointy hats and shiny noisemakers. Especially when the initial policyholder saw how much these settlements could be worth in good, old-fashioned, hard cash. The big bonus was that, unlike viaticals, the insured didn't have to be dying to cash in, and that really is a whole lot nicer, isn't it? The policy sellers could actually live long enough to spend that money on mortgage payments or medical expenses or trips to the fjords or fresh flowers or parties with pointy hats ... whatever. It didn't matter. It was their money, free and clear of restrictions, to do with as they wanted.

Well, it is perhaps no surprise that this idea went over famously well. Investors had a whole vast new world of potential policies to buy and were no longer restricted to scrounging around for policyholders already stricken by fatal illness. Policyholders had a way to make a big heap of money they hadn't really counted on getting, and all just for selling something they might well have gotten rid of for next to nothing. By the time the new millennium was in full swing, these arrangements were being spread across the country like butter melting on toast. And because they differed a bit from viaticals with regard to the insured's life expectancy, and because the insurance industry loves nothing more than confusing people by giving different names to the same thing, these arrangements came to be known as *life settlements*.

Life Settlements and the Changes They Hath Wrought

With the precedent of viatical laws and regulations already set, the legal establishment was quicker to respond to life settlements than they had been with viaticals. Existing state viatical laws were sometimes massaged into applying to life settlement transactions. In 2001, NAIC expanded the Model

Act, originally only applicable to viaticals, so that it could apply to all sales of life insurance policies to the secondary market and not just those made by terminally ill policyholders. In some cases where the old viatical statutes just didn't work, new state-based regulations began to hit the books. At the end of the day, regulators in most states were largely able to prevent another round of Wild West-type dirty tricks from re-contaminating a marketplace that had so recently been detoxified.

Life settlements got so hot so fast that they quickly spawned a sizeable secondary industry of their own. The providers (institutional investors) who had once specialized in viaticals broadened their scope to include the purchase of life settlements, but the potential market was so much bigger it could easily support more dedicated providers. These continued to pop up until there were suddenly dozens of dedicated life settlement providers on the scene.

As the number of players in the life settlement market continued to increase, life settlement transactions themselves became more sophisticated. In the first days of viaticals, the transaction was always between a single viator and a single, individual, private investor. When investment firms and full-time viatical providers joined the party, viaticals between a viator and an institutional provider became much more common. After life settlements made their grand entrance, settlors almost always sold their policies to institutional providers. A direct transaction between a policyholder and a single, individual investor was mostly a relic of the past.

(Yeah, you noticed we tried to sneak a new term in on you there. A *settlor* is exactly the same as a viator in a viatical transaction—that is, the person insured by the policy being sold. And no, that's not a spelling error. In a life settlement, it's "settlor," with an "o," not "settler," with an "e." Investment guys have so much money, they can even change spelling rules.)

Now, this institutional investing brought with it a ravenous appetite for policies. A larger portfolio of policies enabled providers to reduce risk by employing *pooling strategies*. What this means in actual English is that institutional providers, unlike individual investors, had the financial wherewithal to buy lots of policies, and only a few of those policies had to pay out to cover the risk of loss on all the others. If a provider has, let's say, 100 policies, it would only take something like ten or maybe even less of those to pay out to cover any loss that might be incurred if the people insured by the other 90 policies all live well past their life expectancies and force additional premium payments. So providers bought up those policies like hotcakes.

The institutional providers also introduced layers of complexity to what once had been a simple transaction. In many cases, life settlement providers still act like the earlier viatical providers—they serve as the end investor in the deal by buying the policy and holding it until maturity. But providers have other tricks up their sleeves. Sometimes, they will resell policies to either individual investors or other investment firms, taking a slice of profit off the resale. Some policies may even be sold and resold a number of times. In other instances, providers will establish a pool of policies, then sell shares of that pool to investors. The institutional presence in the secondary market had not only made it bigger, but smarter, too.

A Star Is Born: The Secondary Life Insurance Market Hits the Big Time

The potential enormity of the life settlement market was the last bait needed to get the biggest of the big investment fish to bite. Before, the heavy hitters had turned their aristocratic noses up at the notion of investing in a market as limited as viaticals. There just weren't that many viatical-eligible life insurance policies to buy and that kept the investment giants from doing the kind of volume that they prefer to do when they jump in on an investment track. Plus, there was all that icky fraud. And there was the whole "investing in death" stigma that viaticals awoke in some people. But once the market showed that it could behave itself and be regulated, once the concept of a secondary life insurance market had gone mainstream, once the potential investment opportunity had been greatly expanded by the increased market size … that's when the big boys began to sing a different tune.

Warren Buffet was one of that tune's first singers. Among the big boys, he was one of the earliest to jump on the bandwagon and publicly champion the virtues of the secondary market. And when Warren sings, you can bet that other investment leaders will start singing, too. And they did. Like the world's strangest gospel choir. One made up entirely of rich, white bankers. But the song they sang was the music of profit; the gospel they preached was a message of money.

To give you some indication of how big this life settlement thing has become, we'll just give you a few of the names that have invested heavily in this space. Of course, there's old friend Warren Buffet's Berkshire Hathaway. Others joining the club: AIG, JP Morgan Chase, Deutsche Bank, and Bear Stearns. Want more? How about Credit Suisse First Boston, the Royal Bank of Scotland, Wells Fargo, and Cantor Fitzgerald. These names, among many others, represent multinational banks, international investment conglomerates, global insurance companies, pension funds, hedge funds, and most other kinds of investment organisms you can imagine. Insurance rating company A.M. Best released a set of official investment guidelines for life settlements. Cantor Fitzgerald has even recently rolled out an online exchange called LexNet for the pricing and auction of potential life settlement policies.

This is a huge step as it represents the first time a major Wall Street firm has attempted to officially commoditize life settlements by making the offers and values for settlements public.

As life settlements gain acceptability as investment vehicles, they are increasingly becoming more commonplace as a means to diversify investment portfolios because their rate of return is not connected to either interest rates or the stock market. In fact, the day may soon be upon us when life settlements are considered a standard and essential factor in any large, well-constructed investment profile.

Maybe you're the kind of person who prefers dollar amounts and statistical figures. Here are some numbers for you. Sanford C. Bernstein & Company has estimated that about $13 billion worth of life insurance policies were purchased by investors in 2005. That's not a typographical error. That's $13 **billion**—with a "B." Maple Life Financial—one among those dozens of dedicated life settlement providers—has produced an even more optimistic number, claiming as much $15 billion of policies were sold to investors in 2005. Bernstein & Co. speculates that this number could hit $160 billion by 2030 depending on whether or not Congress decides to eliminate the estate tax. (As we mentioned earlier in this book, lots of people own high-value life insurance policies just to pay off these taxes. If they are eliminated, the policyholders might decide they don't need their policies anymore and sell them on the market.) James Camper, Regional Vice President at the market-leading life settlement firm The Coventry Group, has stated that the current number of eligible policies in force indicates a viable market worth as much as $200 billion.

Yep. Our little market is all grown up now. And we remember when it was just knee-high to a grasshopper.

They do grow up so fast …

The Policy Pageant: What Providers Are Looking For and What Your Policy Is Worth

When the big investment firms came to the life settlement market, they didn't quietly creep in the back door. They came with trumpets blaring and guns blazing. Many of them bought out smaller firms that specialized in the life settlement space. Others staffed up with grizzled secondary market veterans who had been around since the market's Wild West days. Most of the big companies dedicated whole arms of their investment machine to handling life settlements. They've committed an incredible amount of time, money and manpower. Why? Because as big as the market already is, they know it's only going to grow in the coming years, and that growth could be explosive.

Nowadays, most life settlement providers are old hats at this game. They cut their teeth on viaticals, made their mistakes, learned their lessons. This stuff has been around for years now; it isn't brand new anymore. Good investment practices have been created based on the things that have been learned and the concepts that have worked. The market is no longer a toddler learning to walk; it's at the Olympics running the 50-yard dash. Providers have changed and refined their approach in many respects and have become much more savvy in judging the differences between a good, safe bet and going all-in at the World Series of Poker with a pair of threes. To put it in old, stodgy investment terminology, life settlement providers have learned how to fine-tune their approach to maximize profit while minimizing risk.

One way they've gone about this is by formalizing their pricing procedure. Long gone are the days when hip, flying-by-the-seat-of-their-pants mavericks bought policies at prices cavalierly calculated from gut feelings, tiny voices in their heads and general whimsy. The pricing process is a rigidly scientific one now. Though different providers may use dissimilar pricing theories and techniques, most begin the pricing process the same way: with a *life expectancy analysis*. Because the words "life expectancy analysis" involve too many syllables, industry types usually sensibly shorten the name to *LE*. Never let it be said that people in the insurance industry aren't efficient.

LEs are pretty much what you'd expect … they're an analysis of a potential settlor's medical records to update that settlor's life expectancy. These LEs are expressed in terms of estimated months left on the clock, so to speak. If a settlor has a life expectancy of exactly twelve years, it would be expressed as 144 months. LEs are usually performed by independent, third-party companies who are contracted by the life settlement providers, though recently many of the larger providers have begun to use proprietary methods to come up with their own in-house LEs. In order for an LE to be performed, the potential settlor must sign a HIPAA compliant authorization to permit access to their medical records. There is no medical exam. We can see you're disappointed.

Life settlement providers then take that LE and use it as a central factor when coming up with a good price for the target policy. A good price is one that is competitive—that is, enticing to the potential settlor—while still low enough to virtually guarantee that the provider (or some other investor) will make a juicy profit on the deal even if the settlor lives a reasonable amount of time past their life expectancy.

The real prize is when a provider finds a low-cost, high-profit policy hidden among an insurance company's books. Buried treasure, let's call it. By attempting to improve on the insurance company's actuarial data, life settlement providers can sometimes find policyholders who should actually be classified as standard but are charged the premium rates of a preferred holder. They may also find someone whose premiums reflect a life expectancy of, say, 120 months, but whose health has actually gone south and really only has an effective life expectancy of 70 months. In both cases, the premium costs are lower than they should be based on the actual condition of the policyholder. Lower costs, same death benefit payout … buried treasure, indeed.

If there's any silver lining at all to contracting some sort of condition that could shorten your lifespan, it's this life insurance policy valuation increase, assuming, of course, that you have a life insurance policy in force. Anything that reduces life expectancy will mean that the policy is worth more to investors, and they will be willing to give you more cash for that policy as a result. Admittedly small consolation, perhaps, but having more money can at least help ease the burden.

The statistical medicine of LE-based pricing isn't the only way providers look to maximize their investment potential. They learned a thing or two about picking the best policies for investment during their early years in the trenches of the secondary market. They used this experience to devise some guidelines on the exact properties they most want to see when they are out trolling for policies to buy for life settlements. As a rule of thumb, these general guidelines don't change a lot from provider to provider. When something works, providers just stick to it.

One thing providers discovered was that it was more important than ever to favor high value policies. Oh, sure, even in the earliest days of viaticals, it was always a whole heck of a lot better to get a high value policy than a lower value one. Hey, more money is more money. But this becomes even more vital for a life settlement. A viatical, by definition, means that there is a very high statistical probability for a payout within two years. The risk to a viatical investor isn't very big … as long as there is no appearance of the much-feared miracle cure syndrome. If a viatical provider isn't wildly reckless by offering far too much money when a policy is bought, that policy is certain to turn a profit.

Not so with a life settlement. No matter how careful and studious an LE may be, there is always a reasonable chance that an insured person will live longer than expected, especially given that today's life expectancies are all trending longer anyway due to improved medications and health care. All those extra years come at a price to an investor paying life insurance premiums, making life settlements more of a risk. Little aggressive investors don't necessarily mind risk. Taking good risks is how little aggressive investors turn into big, hulking investors. But big, hulking investors don't much care for risk anymore. They've matured past all that risky kid's stuff. When those big investment firms take a risk, it better darn well be worth their while.

And with the life settlement market increasingly under the control of big investment firm providers, it means that only high value policies will usually get looked at for potential purchase.

Translation: Today's life settlement providers will almost never look at a life insurance policy with a death benefit value of less than $250,000. Some claim to buy policies worth as little as $100,000. For the most part, they won't. If, however, you already have a policy worth somewhere between $100,000 and $250,000, it probably doesn't hurt to float it past a few providers to see if you get any nibbles.

Another thing investors had learned the hard way was that the life expectancy for older policyholders was more reliable than it was for younger folks. Well, duh. When we get older, the likelihood that we will pass on each additional year increases far more than it does for a young person. The closer we get to the end of our projected run here on this planet, the more accurately a medical analyst can guess when that run is going to end. But the surprise was that even the mortality for younger people suffering from the same life-threatening condition could be very different. As a result, providers favored the life insurance policies of elderly folks, because their life expectancies were much more predictable.

Translation: Unless you are someone who has been diagnosed with a terminal illness or condition and have a life expectancy of less than two (maybe three) years, you will not be able to sell your life insurance policy unless you are at least 65 years old. 70 years old or more is better.

So the investment world has a pretty good handle now on what works and what doesn't. They know exactly what kind of policies they want—policies worth $250,000 or more belonging to settlors 65 years of age or older. They also have pricing procedures based on solid, actuarial principles. While the specific pricing techniques may vary between providers, the general factors that influence the price of a policy are:

- The policy's face value—Obviously, the higher the face value, the better the price.

- The settlor's life expectancy—The shorter the life expectancy, the better the price. Boiling it down, the older the settlor is, the higher the price will be for the policy. Also, the more severe a settlor's diagnosed health conditions are, the more valuable the policy. (Though if the settlor's life expectancy is below two years, the transaction will be a viatical rather than a life settlement.) For example, the policy of someone diagnosed with a congenital heart defect will be worth more than someone whose policy is the same in all other ways, but does not have the heart defect.

- The type of policy—The price for the policy will be different depending on whether it is whole life, variable life, universal life, convertible term, etc. Universal life is generally the most desirable and so will usually fetch the highest price. Furthermore, additional policy riders and guarantees may also impact the price offer.

- Premium costs for the policy—The lower the premium costs, the better the price a settlor can expect to get.

- The policy's existing cash value—The more cash value a policy has built up, the higher the price will be.

- The rating of the issuing insurance company—The higher the rating of the insurance company that issued the policy, the more that policy may be worth.

Driven by investor experience and actuarial science, the life settlement machine began to purr along quite nicely. When the big boys stepped into the game, they brought with them even more stability, new market legitimacy and the highest standards of fiscal discipline. The secondary market had cut its long hair and gone corporate. It got press coverage. And the more press it got, the more public it became. The more public it became, the more mainstream it went. The more mainstream it went, the more investors just kept flocking to it in droves. So the market kept getting bigger and bigger and bigger …

And that's when it hit a real problem. An implacable, unyielding, unconquerable, undeniable, impossible brick wall of a problem.

The market was running out of policies to buy.

Again.

6

The Battle Begins: The Birth of Non-Recourse Premium Financing

And so it was that from the far corners of the land came the same forlorn cry:

"Policies! We need your life insurance policies! Pleeease!"

Life settlement agents slumped by the doors of senior centers in rumpled Armani suits with cardboard signs hung around their necks that read: "Will work for policies."

Life settlement providers threw their hands up to the heavens and prayed to the great gods of investment returns that they might have mercy upon them and favor them with towering stacks of glittering new life insurance policies. ("And if it's not too much trouble, oh great gods of investment returns, could you by chance make them universal life policies worth $10 million or more from people at least 85 years old? Amen.")

But no more policies appeared.

And good policies for investment got harder and harder to find. Like in the old days of viaticals, the marketplace was being picked clean. The investor market had grown into a hulking, hungry monster with glowing dollar signs for eyes and a ravenous, insatiable appetite for life insurance policies.

In order to satisfy the expanding secondary market, in order for life settlement promoters and agents to continue to thrive, someone would have to do something drastic to fuel this giant machine.

Someone had to feed the monster.

The Johnny Appleseed Effect

The problem was that there was only a finite number of policies in force out there. Of these, only a smattering had the ideal characteristics that investors were really looking for, namely policies worth at least $250,000 owned by people over 70 years of age. Providers occasionally stretched the bounds of what they would consider ideal by condescending to buy policies valued at less than $250,000 from people as young as 65. But they weren't really happy about doing this. All those years of investing in the secondary market had taught them what turned a worthwhile profit. Anything else came with too much risk or too much overhead and was more trouble than it was worth.

What the life settlement market really needed was more policyholders.

No, wait …

What it really, *really* needed was more policyholders over 70 years old with policies worth $1 million or more.

Yep … That'd sure be nice. If only there was a way to get more good policies in the game …

See, there were lots of people who fit the demographic that life settlement providers were looking for. Lots and lots of people were over 70 years of age, and quite a few of them had a net worth of more than a million bucks. The problem was that most of these people didn't have life insurance policies. An advertising push to convince these folks to buy life insurance was doomed to fail because most of them just didn't see life insurance as a necessary asset anymore. Their need-based reasons for having life insurance had run their course. Heck, some might even have already surrendered or lapsed policies they used to have. Plus, the many who had never heard of a secondary market for life insurance were understandably reluctant to spend their own money to buy a policy for a transaction that, frankly, sounded too good to be true. And those who were familiar with the secondary market might well have heard of the fraud that was prevalent during the viatical years—a poor track record that scared away some of the more informed potential settlors.

With so many good reasons for these folks *not* to buy life insurance, the grim mission of life settlement promoters and agents was to figure out some way to convince them to pick up new life insurance policies they didn't believe they needed so that providers could buy them and keep the life settlement ball rolling.

This concept was called *seeding*, and conceptually it was a lot like recruiting. If promoters could find a way to make buying life insurance painless, enticing and worry-free, it would swell the ranks of policyholders. Plant enough new trees, there would eventually be plenty of apples for everybody. Seed enough new policies, there just might be enough to satisfy the policy-eating market monster.

But what to do? How could life settlement agents recruit more ideal candidates to buy life insurance?

Intriguing Insurable Interest Issues Involving Investors

One surefire way for the life settlement industry to bring in new policyholders was to pay for the policies themselves. That was certain to go over big. All a provider really had to do was have a representative approach a candidate who fit the ideal life settlor profile, offer that candidate a big ole' pile of money for the trouble of applying for insurance, pay all the premiums for the candidate's life insurance policy, sign themselves on as the beneficiary of that person's policy, then wait to collect. It didn't take a whiz to figure that out, and the life settlement industry was full to bursting with high-power financial wizards who could've conjured up more complex schemes in a coma. As long as the investor's LE and actuarial data were sound, there ought to be good profit with minimal risk, and the insured would get his or her mound of money, too. It was beautifully simple and perfectly delightful. So what's the problem?

Well, the problem is a legal one. Many of the laws that come into play during a life settlement transaction are life insurance regulations that deal specifically with the concept of *insurable interest*. While we'll get into the specific legal issues surrounding it life insurance secondary market a little later in this book, it is important to have a grasp of what insurable interest is in order to understand why the life settlement market went about things the way they did. Suffice it to say for now that insurable interest laws came about as a result of some nefarious practices with regard to life insurance policies that were carried out back in 18th century England. Chief among these was a tendency for strangers to go out and buy a life insurance policy on someone they had never met without the insured person's knowledge. It meant that people were walking around with giant price tags on their heads, and they never even knew it. Needless to say, "accidents" were frequent. The insurable interest laws were created to curtail this sort of monkey business and legitimize the zoo that the life insurance industry had become. Those laws passed in England were then brought over here to the United States where they became the basis for state laws governing life insurance behavior.

While the precise legal definition of insurable interest is something that is still being thrashed out today—sometimes viciously—in court cases all around the country, it is fairly safe to say that a few characteristics have more or less been agreed upon:

- The insured person must produce written consent before a policy can be made active.

- If the person buying a policy is not the insured person, then the buyer must have an insurable interest in the insured. That is, the buyer must enjoy a reasonable economic advantage from the continued life of the insured. This could mean a spouse or dependents. But it could also mean a business partner whose financial security depends on the insured. In some cases, it could mean an unmarried domestic partner, too, though these cases are still up in the air at the moment.

■ Finally, while insurable interest must be demonstrated at the time of policy purchase, it doesn't have to exist when the death benefit is paid.

Sooo … what does this all mean? Bottom line: Investors can't just go out and buy insurance for someone else. However, if someone goes out and buys their own insurance, they have the right to transfer ownership of that policy to whomever they choose.

That's not to say that less scrupulous life settlement agents never tried to buy policies for people. In the market's wild, foolhardy youth, there were cases where investors either footed the bill for a settlors's premiums or fronted money to the settlor for those premiums. Wherever these were discovered, insurable interest laws were employed by the insurance company to either rescind the policy or gleefully deny the death benefit claim. These cases were given their own names by the insurance industry: *Stranger Owned Life Insurance (SOLI)* or *Investor Owned Life Insurance (IOLI)*. When SOLI/IOLI cases first started hitting the courts, they often referred to the illegal practice described above—where an investor had paid for the premiums for a new policy from the outset. Legal challenges in these specific situations were just about always won by the insurance company. And when a challenge was successful, it was invariably the investor who took it on the chin.

So the life settlement industry quickly figured out that buying the policy outright wasn't going to work, but how 'bout this one: the settlor shells out his or her own money for the first premium, so it clearly belongs to him or her. Then, the settlor can turn around right away and transfer ownership to a life settlement provider. The policy would not technically have been *issued* to a provider but would have been *transferred* to a provider—a right that is permitted under almost all legal interpretations of insurable interest laws. How does that sound?

Not too good, said the insurance companies, shaking their collective heads. Not too good at all.

Punching and Counterpunching with the Contestability Clause

The main problem with this heady approach is that it runs afoul of the contestability clause. You may remember from chapter 3 that this clause is part of every life insurance contract. It indicates that the insurance company can rub out a policy for just about any legal reason within the first two years of coverage. After two years, things get a lot tougher for an insurance company from a legal standpoint. If it wants to rescind a policy or deny a claim then, it must demonstrate a case for willful fraud, a much heavier legal burden of proof.

A policy that is still within its first two years in force is called a *wet* policy; a policy older than two years is a *seasoned* policy. Anytime a policy is sold on the secondary life insurance market while it's still wet, it's called a *wet ink deal* or a *wet paper deal*. From an investor's perspective, a wet ink deal is a dive off a 40-foot cliff into a kiddie pool. You might be okay, but chances are considerably better that it'll ruin your day. If an insurance company sees that a policy changes hands to a life settlement provider while it's still in its contestable period … blow the whistle—the game's over. Whenever an insurance company sniffs out a SOLI/IOLI deal during those first two years of policy ownership, it will often rescind the policy on the grounds that it was secured with the intent to sell to an investor rather than for traditional need-based reasons.

This was another lesson the life settlement market discovered the hard way. Investors lost millions of dollars due to the rescinding of wet ink policies, so they generally learned to steer clear of them. While wet ink deals are still out there today, they are exclusively the domain of small investors capitalizing on the fact that they don't have to fight with the big investment powers for policies belonging to people who are looking to "flip," or quick sell, their policies right after getting them. Less competition means lower prices, so these small investors can buy these wet policies for less money than they would cost when they're seasoned. But it's a spectacularly enormous risk. For the most part, you can count on the fact that a life settlement transaction today will only be conducted with a seasoned policy.

At this point, you might be catching a trend here. The back and forth between the life insurance secondary market and the insurance companies is a lot like one of the elaborate sword fights in those Errol Flynn movies. Jab-thrust-parry-jump on a table-counterthrust-parry-swing from the chandelier-kick-thrust … It's a dangerous dance of profit, with each side bringing armies of grizzled lawyers wielding laws like scythes. And with each clash there were casualties—investors claiming losses, insurance companies claiming losses, life settlement providers claiming unfair and illegal business practices, insurance companies claiming the same. Life insurance had become a blood sport, complete with name-calling and trash-talking.

How in the world did this get so ugly? Why are insurance companies so dead set against these transactions? Why do they fight so hard to destroy them? After all, couldn't this ultimately be a boon for the industry? The existence of the secondary market could suddenly make lots of people who didn't really want life insurance before rush out to buy it. That means more premium revenue for the industry. And with their many decades of actuarial data behind them, insurance companies know what to charge on their premiums to turn a profit on a policy no matter what the applicant's circumstances. If there is no expectation of profiting or the risk is too high ... why, the applicant simply wouldn't clear the underwriting and the company just won't sell the insurance. So is the industry being unreasonable? Stubborn? Grouchy?

Why in the heck are insurance companies so darn ornery about this thing?

Insurance Companies Don't Get Mad, They Get Even: Why the Industry Dislikes the Secondary Market

Truth be told, insurance companies were never happy with this whole secondary market business. And why should they be? They spent centuries perfecting their mortality tables and actuarial models. They had all that history and experience, cabinets full of yellowing policy records and bookcases creaking under stacks of dusty old tomes, each page filled to bursting with information that made their profitable business an even more profitable one. Every line in those pages, every piece of code in the actuarial computer software was meticulously crafted to take the gamble out of the game. What insurance companies didn't want was change. All that history, all that data ... it just doesn't amount to a hill of baked beans if someone keeps changing the rules. And those rules had made the insurance industry one of the most profitable businesses on this fine planet of ours.

The life insurance industry started getting itchy all the way back in those first days of viaticals. When the viatical investors created the secondary market by diving into the pool of potential viator policies, they sent waves rippling right over the heads of insurance companies who had been serenely floating along for over a hundred years. No one had ever applied market-value principles to in-force policies before. The insurance industry came up indignant and sputtering.

By making its accelerated death benefits more readily available and more competitive with market prices, the insurance industry offered its first salvo of return fire, an indication that the giant had opened its eyes and was more than a little irritated at having its century-long slumber interrupted by a bunch of pipsqueak investors.

For a while, these improved ADBs were enough to quiet the roaring mouse. The insurance industry was back in control. And things were just the way they ought to be, as far as insurance companies were concerned.

That is, until life settlements strode into the spotlight.

Life settlements were a whole new headache. While viaticals were as irritating as a mosquito in the bedroom, there was a limited market. The number of policies that investors could buy that were suitable for viatical transactions was self-restricting by its very nature. And as the medical community started getting the AIDS epidemic under some level of control, and as insurance companies cut deeply into viatical sales through ADBs, the viatical industry was reduced to a small nuisance buzzing in the dark.

Ah, but life settlements ...

They changed everything.

Remember all those stacks of yellowing papers and books, those decades of mortality tables and actuarial data? Remember how they're used extensively to determine the proper premium costs? Along with underwriting techniques, those actuary-based pricing schedules pretty much comprise the entire life insurance biz in a tidy nutshell. That stuff is why insurance companies make such a hefty profit in an industry built entirely on risk.

Life settlements took those numbers, those years of calculations and expertise and effort, and threw them out the window.

Okay, maybe that's an exaggeration, but not as much of one as you might think.

Take Your Hands Off Our Lapse Rate

The trouble with life settlements has to do with the notion of an investor owning another person's life insurance policy. Under more traditional circumstances, a policyholder will often see their need for insurance diminish as they age. As this happens, policyholders tend to surrender their policies. Insurance companies can't help but find these policy lapses positively delightful. While the insurance company has to return the cash value (minus surrender charges, of course), all those payments covering the net amount at risk were pure profit. The only expense from the insurance company's perspective was operational overhead, because there was never any payout of the death benefit. And those death benefits can be a real bummer of an expense.

In the life insurance industry, the rate at which people stop paying their premiums before the payment of the death benefit is called the *lapse rate*. For the math geeks among us, the lapse rate is the number of policies canceled during a fixed period of time divided by the number of policies in force at the beginning of that period.

The lapse rate was always a tricky little bird for the industry to handle. It can fluctuate quite a bit based on external economic conditions; if things are bad out there, lots of folks can't afford their life insurance premiums and let their coverage lapse. Paradoxically, this can be a good thing for life insurance companies. Still, it can get dicey. If a policyholder lapses too early, there might not be enough premium income to cover the overhead expense associated with initiating that policy. If a policyholder never lapses, well, then the insurance company has to pay out that death benefit, and it really isn't fond of that notion at all. If too many people lapse, then there is a substantial drop in premium revenue; if too few lapse, there are too many death benefit payouts and the insurance company takes a profit hit that way. It's like a ballerina balancing delicately on her toes. The slightest push and the poor girl will topple over. Life settlements weren't a slight push … they were like getting hit by a truck.

How do life settlements impact lapse rate, you might ask. It comes down to who's holding the policy. If it's a regular Joe or Jane, their need for insurance usually diminishes as they get older. They also might suffer times of economic hardship. Statistics have shown that many life insurance policies never pay out a death benefit. A large portion of policyholders wind up lapsing their coverage or surrendering their policy to collect the accumulated cash value later in life. According to the American Council of Life Insurers Fact Book from 2006, about 7.6% of all policies were voluntarily terminated in 2006. With this kind of annual lapse rate, very few in force policies will survive to maturation.

If a policy is owned by an investor, however, an insurance company can count on that policy never, ever, ever lapsing. An investor doesn't own a policy for need-based reasons; that policy is an investment. And that investment isn't worth a penny of profit unless and until it pays that death benefit. Come hell, high water, or invasion by space aliens, those premiums will be paid.

So here we have this insurance industry, cruising along comfortably with all this actuarial data compiled from many years of experience. The elusive lapse rate has been calculated through painstaking analysis, and it has been applied as a major factor in determining the premiums policyholders will pay across the board. Along come life settlements. The lapse rate plummets as more and more investors get in the game. More and more death benefits get paid out. The insurance industry sees its profit margins go down. Its premium pricing is now out of whack. An industry that dislikes change is suddenly reeling from it. It's unhappy. It wants to put a stop to this nonsense in the worst way.

And that's when, lest there be any hope for peace, some in the rapidly growing life settlement industry took one more shot at the insurance companies. Their attempts to seed new policies were bringing in older policyholders. An older policyholder is closer to a death benefit payout with the possibility of many fewer premium payments coming in before then. Sure, actuarial data had determined the much higher premiums these folks would have to pay to keep their policies profitable from the company's perspective, but the actuarial data and premium payment structure had been thrown into pandemonium by the impact of life settlements on the lapse rate. Insurance companies were having a hard time determining who was profitable or what to charge. And these older customers were not desirable from the insurance company's perspective. They were high risk, and insurance companies hate risk. On any given day, these new customers were much more likely to require a death benefit payout than a 35-year-old head of household with a family of four. And the insurance books were getting clogged by new policyholders who fit this high-risk profile. In addition, there was some political risk beginning to surface. Life insurance products enjoy some very unusual and favorable tax benefits – such as (in most cases) a tax free death benefit and tax favored growth and withdrawal of the cash surrender values. If all of a sudden the industry was dominated by slick investors, receiving death proceeds, instead of families and businesses, would the tax benefits come under attack by the government? No one can be sure of the answer, but the mere possibility of the loss of these benefits is enough to scare insurance company executives up to the highest levels.

It was the last straw.

The giant was ready for war.

The Rise of Non-Recourse Premium Financing: It Came From Beneath a Bank ...

Remember now, life settlement agents were still looking for ways to seed new policies. You know, to feed the policy-eating secondary market monster. They just had to find a way to do it while tiptoeing around the angry giant.

So they thought and they thought. But everything they came up with, every way they turned, there was an obstacle. On one hand were the lawyer armies of the angry giant waving around weapons forged from insurable interest laws. On the other was an aging target base who found themselves reluctant to pay their own money to buy something they didn't much want just for the chance to sign up for a concept as unusual and too-good-to-be-true-sounding as a life settlement transaction.

What to do?

When inspiration finally struck, it hit life settlement agents like a bolt of lightning from a cloudless sky. It seemed those old gods of investment returns had heard their pleas, after all. But when the bolt of inspiration came, it really came from another industry entirely.

A number of people in the life settlement industry either worked for banks, in banks, or with banks. One glance back to chapter 5 at the list of the sorts of investors involved in life settlements will reveal just how prominent a role the banking industry plays in today's secondary market for life insurance.

That means there is a whole gaggle of experienced banking officials with their feet firmly buried in the sand of both the life settlement and banking industries. These guys approached the seeding issue by taking a page right out of the banking playbook; they offered ideal, potential life settlors who did not currently have life insurance the chance to finance the purchase of a new policy through the use of a *non-recourse loan*.

To someone unfamiliar with them, a non-recourse loan can seem like a peculiar sort of creature. It operates quite a bit differently from the more usual bank loans. In a non-recourse loan, the lending agent allows a person or organization to borrow money to finance some project or property transaction. The loan is paid back only from the revenue generated by that project or transaction; the borrower does not have to send in regular payments to pay off the loan as would be the case with a more typical loan like a mortgage.

A loan with no payment schedule? Hey, sounds positively dreamy. Until the non-recourse loan is paid off, however, it accrues interest just like any normal loan, so the balance keeps getting bigger and bigger. And there is a set amount of time called the *loan period* at the end of which the loan must be paid off. If the project or property transaction fails to cover the cost of the loan by then, that's when things really get interesting …

The only collateral in a non-recourse loan is the project or property funded by that loan. If the borrower defaults on the loan, the lender can seize the collateral. But that's where it all ends. The lender can't go after any of the borrower's other assets. If the value of the seized project or property fails to cover the full loan, the lender is out the difference and out of luck. The lender assumes all risk. That's why non-recourse loans are called non-recourse loans. The lender has … well … no recourse should the borrower be unable to hold up their end of the deal. Typically, these loans have a high interest rate—often up around the high teens or so. Those high rates are a big part of what makes these sorts of arrangements attractive to the lender. Also, the lender takes great care to make sure that the collateralizing property is valuable enough to make the loan risk worthwhile.

An example of a non-recourse loan in action would be your typical real estate development deal, a transaction often funded by this sort of loan. A developer would take out a non-recourse loan to buy a piece of property, using that piece of property as collateral for the loan. They'd then develop that property—they're probably building condos … developers just love condos. Once the developer starts selling those condo units, they can start paying off the loan with the proceeds. However, if everything falls through and the borrower can't pay the loan by the end of the loan period, there's no need for the borrower to hoof it out of town to El Salvador to avoid having their other assets attacked. All the lender can do is seize that loan-funded property purchase to try to recoup its losses, usually by turning it around and selling it on the open market.

Now let's bring this odd sort of loan to the brave new world of life settlement transactions. If a viable applicant with an ideal profile (read: a person over 70 worth at least a million bucks) wants to participate in a life settlement transaction, they would be able to buy a brand, spanking new policy without laying out a penny of their own cash by using a non-recourse loan. Even though the loan would be set up by a life settlement agent, the insured person would still be the owner of the policy because the loan is in their name, thereby skirting any problem with insurable interest laws. Because there is no cash outlay and because the policy itself will serve as the non-recourse loan's only collateral, there is no financial risk to the settlor. And since the settlor isn't actually paying out-of-pocket for anything, it's not a problem to hang onto the policy for two years to season it past the contestability period. When it's all said and done, you wind up with a solution that gets around insurable interest laws, while providing an attractive, risk-free proposition to potential applicants. Plus, settlors get the impression that they're getting those two years of insurance "free," because they're not paying for them out-of-pocket.

Pretty slick, huh?

We told you those life settlement people were sharp.

Roger's Tale: A Case Study of a Non-Recourse Premium Financing Transaction

To really get a good look at how one of these *non-recourse premium financing* arrangement works, let's go through a step-by-step example and see how it all fits together.

Let's suppose we have a friend named Roger. Roger is 74 years old. During those 74 years, he hasn't picked up any serious illnesses and never smoked, but he's had more than his share of vodka martinis and would never imagine breaking into a jog unless he was being chased by a tiger. He doesn't have a life insurance policy, but he's heard all this noise about life settlements and selling your policy and such, and he wants to join the party.

His first step is to go to an insurance agent who also brokers life settlements. The agent then invites Roger to fill out a small but somewhat intimidating array of forms. These forms will include a general questionnaire that asks probing questions about his net worth, a health history questionnaire and a HIPAA form that permits access to his private medical records. The agent will send the medical information along to a life expectancy company or two, who will eventually return an LE analysis. All of this taken together will give the agent a good picture of Roger's potential success as a life settlement candidate.

Now let's say it's all systems go for our buddy, Roger. He's got the green light from the life settlement agent. The agent then tries to secure the best possible life insurance rate, meaning that he's looking to get a policy with the highest possible face value for the lowest possible premium cost given Roger's current insurance capacity. Roger's got a net worth of around $6 million or thereabouts, so the agent is able to find an insurance company willing to offer him a $5 million standard issue universal life policy with an annual premium of $225,000. That's a heck of a nice policy and a very reasonable premium given Roger's age, his risk classification and the policy's value. Time to stand and applaud. Our life settlement agent deserves an ovation for this one.

So now we know what the cost of this arrangement would be. In order to season the policy past the contestability period, Roger would have to hold onto it for two years. That means two years of life insurance coverage. That's fine, but given his life circumstances Roger isn't much interested in that coverage, and he's reluctant to hand out the $450,000 in premium costs that would be required to keep the policy in force for two years. Rather than try to convince Roger to purchase the insurance himself, the life settlement agent suggests the easier way: a non-recourse loan.

He sells Roger on the idea, so the agent then contacts a lending institution that is interested in working with these transactions. There are plenty of them. And why not? It's actually pretty risk-free. The lending institution—let's just call it a bank here—will offer a high interest loan to finance two years' worth of premium payments with only the policy itself as collateral. In this case, that means it's a $450,000 loan—the annual premium of $225,000 times two for the two years of coverage. The bank offers an annual interest rate of 18.7%; that's a high rate, but it's par for the course with a non-recourse loan. Based on that rate, Roger will owe $634,036 at the end of the two-year loan period. That's a heavy price for a two-year $450,000 loan.

Here's the good news: Roger will probably never have to pay that money. Here's why ...

After two years are up, the agent will approach providers to see if any are interested in buying Roger's policy. Given Roger's age and the high face value of his policy, it will probably be an easy sell. In fact, there will probably be an opportunity to compare multiple offers and pick the best one. Each time the policy piques a provider's interest, it will field an offer to the life settlement agent, who will, in turn, present this offer to Roger. If he's happy with the offer, he'll go ahead and give his approval to have the policy's ownership transferred to the investor. Good times for everybody.

Now, in the event that no buyers are found—unlikely as that may be in this case—Roger has two options available to him:

- Pay the loan (and interest) off in full out of his own pocket. This would mean a payment of $634,036 in this instance. If Roger elects to do this, he will retain full ownership of the policy and will continue his life insurance coverage for as long as he decides to pay the premiums to keep it in force. He can keep the insurance until death as a traditional life insurance investment for his assigned beneficiaries, or he can just keep it in force himself with an eye for the market. As he ages, his projected life expectancy will decrease, and the policy will become more attractive to the marketplace. Eventually, someone will want to buy it.

- Default on the loan. If Roger's policy doesn't get any nibbles in the secondary market right away, he may decide that he doesn't want to absorb the expense of keeping the policy in force, no matter how much profit there could be down the road. As a result, Roger would simply not pay the loan when the loan period is up, and the bank would collect its collateral on the loan—namely, the policy. Roger would owe nothing else because the loan is non-recourse. The bank would then either try to sell the policy on the market itself or simply keep it as its own investment.

Okay, let's rewind a bit. We have an insurance quote for a policy for Roger and we have a bank willing to open a non-recourse loan to pay for that policy. Roger must then fill out the application for insurance—complete with an annoying medical exam—and lists someone close to him—a spouse, a son or daughter, another next-of-kin or perhaps an estate trust—as his beneficiary. The process gets put on hold while everyone waits breathlessly for confirmation that Roger's insurance is active and in force. When that confirmation comes in, there's a party at the life settlement agent's office, festive but subdued and tasteful. Okay, not really. But there's a party in spirit.

Two years pass.

They go by so very quickly.

Roger is pleased to find he hasn't died. He's still happily sipping vodka martinis by the pool while playing a mean game of pinochle. If he had passed away, however, here's how all parties would've made out on the deal:

- The beneficiaries Roger assigned when he applied for the policy would have received the full death benefit, from which the loan would have to be paid. That translates to the $5 million death benefit minus the $634,036 loan (that figure includes the interest) resulting in a final death benefit payout of $4,365,964.

- The bank gets its high interest on the loan as its profit, resulting in a tidy sum of $184,036. In most non-recourse premium financing deals, the lender also gets a piece of the insurance commission, usually just around half of it to be exact. In the case of Roger's policy, the total commission is $202,000, meaning the lender would also get an additional $101,000. The final net for the bank, then, would be a profit of $285,036, a nice return for a mere two-year $450,000 loan.

- In a case like this where the applicant passes away before a life settlement transaction can take place, the agent would only get half of the insurance commission for his part in selling Roger the policy, or $101,000. This is why some life settlement agents ask for an upfront fee equal to 1% or .5% of the policy's face value to come out of the applicant's pocket at the outset of the process. It guarantees that the effort will be worth their while. However, the trend has been to do away with this sort of cash upfront fee.

But, as we mentioned, Roger is not dead and is quite happy about it; he is alive and well and playing pinochle by the pool. So now comes the moment of truth. Roger's policy is seasoned and ready for the market. The life settlement agent puts the call out to see if there are any takers. This is too good an opportunity for providers to pass up as it is a $5 million policy for a fellow who is now 76 years old. There are several bids, the best of which comes from a hedge fund manager who offers $1,045,000. This sounds plenty good to Roger and his agent. The deal is done. There is great rejoicing.

Next, the non-recourse loan is paid off from the settlement. That means that of the $1,045,000 received from the hedge fund provider, $634,000 goes toward paying off the loan plus its accrued interest. The rest—$461,000— is profit. It's common in a transaction such as this for the life settlement agent to receive one-third of the life settlement profit and for the client to receive the remaining two-thirds. These percentages may vary depending on the arrangements made with the agent and the amounts involved, but let's assume the very common one-third/two-thirds rule here. With this in mind, here's how everybody made out on this transaction:

- Roger gets two-thirds of the life settlement profit after the loan is paid off. That's $307,333.

- The bank gets the interest profit from the loan—$184,036—plus half of the insurance commission for the sale of the policy—$101,000—for a total profit of $285,036.

- The life settlement agent gets one-third of the settlement profit—$153,667—plus half of the insurance commission for the sale of the policy—$101,000—for a total profit of $254,667.

- The hedge fund provider gets the policy. When Roger passes on, the provider will get the $5 million death benefit payout. Take out the cost of the life settlement and you get a figure of $3,955,000. Take from that each year of premiums that Roger is still alive, and you get the final profit for the provider. In order for that hedge fund to lose money on the transaction, Roger would have to live another 18 years to the age of 93. Possible, certainly—especially given today's improvements in medicine—but statistically unlikely. Plus, Roger really is much too fond of those vodka martinis. That just can't be good for him, can it?

So that's the end of Roger's tale. It seems to have a nice ending. We watch as Roger sails off into the sunset in a new boat, with a crowd of his pinochle friends on board laughing and singing naughty songs. Looks like they've all had too many vodka martinis today. But here's the thing … As pleased with himself as our friend Roger is, he could have done better. How, you might ask. Well, he could've made a lot more money. Later, we'll show you what he should have done.

But Roger doesn't know this. He's pleased as punch and walking on clouds right now. And everyone else—the life settlement agent, the lender, the provider—did awfully well, too. How often do you see a game with no losers? This non-recourse premium financing stuff is a no-brainer, right? A win/win/win all the way around. Hooray! It's candy and popcorn for everybody …

Except for one …

The insurance company.

The angry giant.

And when an angry giant doesn't get its candy …

Look out.

7

The Evolving Art of the Deal: New Seeding Techniques Emerge

Maybe you've seen some of those old westerns where some stranger walks into a boisterous bar, says something inappropriate, and the whole bar falls deathly silent. All the patrons turn to stare at the unfortunate newcomer, and you just know that the poor fellow doesn't have much time left before some offended bar patron who just happens to be an ace gunfighter puts a bullet in his ear.

Wanna see that in real life?

Go into a life insurance company and say this magic phrase ...

Non-recourse premium financing.

Then duck.

Because saying those words to a life insurance executive is an awful lot like smacking an angry bull in the nose with a red flag. But when some crazed insurance actuary is chasing you with a fully loaded staple gun, don't say we didn't warn you ...

Non-Recourse Premium Financing: Is It So Wrong?

In one fell swoop, non-recourse premium financing had taken the legal high ground previously enjoyed by the insurance industry and cast it into shades of gray. A host of life settlement promoters were sneaking around insurable interest laws with ease now, and the insurance industry—our angry giant—responded the way you would expect an angry giant to respond ... by swinging its mighty fists. In this case, its mighty fists were made of legal challenges and court orders. But legal challenges weren't often successful against this slippery, new non-recourse tactic. In state after state, it increasingly became a legally sanctioned—though perhaps not especially well-loved—practice.

It's important to note here that not everyone in the life settlement industry endorsed these non-recourse transactions. Many life settlement proponents disliked the deals and agreed with the insurance industry that they were designed entirely for the purpose of dodging insurable interest laws. Some life settlement providers refused to purchase policies that were financed in this manner. But, unfortunately, there were many warhawks in the insurance industry's camp who refused to see any legal distinction between the usual life settlement transactions and those that involved a non-recourse-driven arrangement. As a result, many of the attacks the insurance companies initiated against the life settlement industry targeted all life settlement transactions and not just those involving non-recourse premium financing seeding techniques.

In fairness, the insurance companies' grouchiness toward non-recourse deals was well-founded. Whether legally supported or not, non-recourse financed life settlements were still making mincemeat out of the life insurance lapse rate. Almost as bad for the insurance companies was that these non-recourse deals were bringing in far too many older policyholders, leading to an increasing number of death benefit payouts. Just because the courts were deciding that these deals were okay didn't mean for a New York minute that the insurance industry approved.

The ideal life insurance policy owner from the insurance company's perspective is a younger person with a long life ahead of them who owns their own policy or the policy of a loved one (i.e., they don't own a stranger's policy). When you consider this, you can see why non-recourse deals were getting so deep under insurance companies' corporate skin. They were pretty much the exact opposite of what the insurance company wanted to see. No matter how you sliced it, a non-recourse deal wound up poking the insurance company in the eye:

- If a life settlor operating under a non-recourse financing deal died within the first two years, the insurance company had to pay out a death benefit without receiving much of anything back in the way of premium payments. That was a stinker of a deal since it always wound up losing the company money.

- If a life settlor lived out the two years then sold the policy to an investor (or turned the policy over as collateral to the non-recourse lender), the insurance company knew darn well that the policy was never going to be lapsed and that eventually it would have to pay that death benefit. The only thing it could hope for here was that the settlor would live long enough to generate enough premiums to more than make up for the cost of the death benefit—an iffy proposition since the settlor in any life settlement is always older and higher risk.

- If the life settlor lived out the two years then bought the policy outright himself or herself, it was usually because there was a downturn in health, and the settlor had decided that he or she did indeed want to provide the assigned beneficiaries with the security of the death benefit. That was bad news for the insurance company, too, since it meant that a death benefit payout was likely coming down the pike in the near future and, once again, was probably going to happen too soon to turn a profit on the policy.

So while non-recourse deals were a win/win/win for everyone else, they were the worst sort of booby prize for the insurance company. Small wonder, then, that insurance companies resented them so.

Small wonder, too, that the insurance industry continued to attack the entire life settlement industry with both barrels blazing. This double-barreled assault came at life settlements in two very different courts—the judicial court and the court of public opinion.

The Two-Pronged Attack

In the life insurance industry, non-recourse premium financing had already become a evil, ugly, nasty phrase, but the insurance industry was hell-bent on making it a dirty phrase for everyone else, too.

This new approach began with the sort of high intensity media blitz normally reserved for celebrity starlets who forgot to wear underpants. Newspapers, magazines and Internet blogs began trotting out stories about "death peddlers" who "gambled on human lives." Insurable interest laws became the new Ten Commandments, carved on stone tablets long ago by long-bearded insurance prophets inspired by divine wisdom. (Although they were written on quite ordinary paper by 18th century Englishmen inspired by pipe tobacco … though they might have had long beards.) All life settlement professionals were characterized as seedy, sweaty people who stalked from shadow to shadow in search of some way to bilk poor insurance companies out of their hard-won profits. And the insurance companies … why, they were martyrs, helpless innocents victimized by calculating individuals dead set on world domination, wholesale destruction, and the systematic slaughter of everything cute and cuddly.

The life insurance industry was asking for sympathy.

How strange.

Among a list of the world's richest, most powerful companies, you'll find insurance companies represented quite well. And for life insurance companies, that substantial quantity of money was made on nothing more or less than "gambling on human lives." That is, after all, precisely what life insurance companies do. That's why actuaries exist—to calculate the odds of those gambles.

The truth was that insurance companies were far less concerned about the supposed ethical issues of life settlements than they were about the fact that these investor interlopers had encroached on their turf, thus monkeying most annoyingly with their lapse rate and premium pricing.

Nevertheless, insurance companies and their advocates did their level best to paint the secondary life insurance market as unethical, gleefully pointing to the fraud that was rampant during the secondary market's earlier viatical days. Of course, they conveniently ignored the fact that in most states the market now had laws and rules to regulate that sort of behavior. Are there still instances of fraud? Absolutely. But there's still fraud in the stock market, too. And that has been around for a far longer period of time, with all those extra years to clean itself up. Guess no one should invest in the stock market, either.

Eventually, the big investment houses and their allies began to rise to the defense of the secondary life insurance market. When Warren Buffet publicly came out in support of life settlements, it opened the floodgates. The investment world's powerful public relations machine began to strike back. A publicity war for hearts and minds was in full swing.

So in the media, the armies of the two sides had found a new battleground, but that didn't mean that they had left the courtrooms in peace. Through the heat and smoke of the public relations war, the struggle for legal precedent continued unabated.

The insurance industry's legal assault went through its own evolution of sorts. First, the definition of SOLI/IOLI cases was expanded to include any instance where the intent from the moment a life insurance policy is issued is to use that policy as an investment vehicle, even if that policy was technically purchased by the insured. Non-recourse transactions and many other life settlement arrangements would then fall under this expanded definition. But while insurance personnel still generally regarded the term "SOLI/IOLI" as describing something filthy, unethical, perhaps even darkly diabolical, the stern ladies and gentlemen of the judicial world ultimately determined that classification as a SOLI/IOLI case didn't really mean one jot from a legal perspective. On the contrary, many found most SOLI/IOLI deals to be fully compliant under current insurance law.

In response, the armies of insurance industry lawyers changed their approach, shifting their focus to the question of ownership. Clearly, someone who bought insurance through a two-year non-recourse loan had no real intention of keeping that insurance beyond the loan period. If they did, they would either pay for the insurance with their own money or use more traditional, lower interest, standard recourse loans to temporarily finance their premium payments—loans which they would pay back out of pocket. And just as clearly, these non-recourse loan arrangements were always made by life settlement companies and investors intent on profiting from that policy. As a result, the insurance industry contended that: 1) because the insured had no real financial investment in the insurance policy; 2) because the insured had little intention of keeping that policy past two years; 3) and because the policy was clearly purchased to benefit those entities and investors who facilitated the deal, the insured's "ownership" of that policy was legally vulnerable.

It was an interesting tack, a reversal of sorts of previous attempts to rewrite insurable interest laws. To reflect this change in direction, some in the insurance industry even began to use new terminology. Classifying non-recourse deals under the header of Stranger Owned Life Insurance or Investor Owned Life Insurance wasn't strictly accurate; the owner of the policy was technically the insured when the policy was issued, even if they only owned it by virtue of the non-recourse loan. More exact terms—*Investor Initiated Life Insurance (IILI)* and *Speculator Initiated Life Insurance (SPINLIFE)*—were devised and used by some to more precisely reflect the nature of a non-recourse transaction.

What the approach really came down to was this: insurance companies wanted people to pay for their own life insurance. We call this the "skin game principle." If an insured had no monetary investment in a policy—no "skin in the game"—it was just too clear that the insured never had any real intent of keeping that policy. In these cases, it was obvious to the insurance company that the policy was going to fall down the rabbit hole into the no-win non-recourse scenario. The industry's holy mandate was to eliminate these profit-eating deals, and it was determined to find a way to do it.

Decidedly Undecided: The Legal Struggle for Ambiguous Clarification

While the judicial onslaught against non-recourse financed policies continued, insurance companies took big steps to tip the scales of justice in their favor. Instead of relying entirely on the mercies of the courts—a strategy that had a less than stellar track record for them to this point—change-phobic insurance companies were reluctantly dragged into making changes. These changes primarily occurred in their underwriting, and the object of these changes was to do everything possible to sniff out policies destined for SOLI/IOLI or IILI or SPINLIFE or whatever-you-want-to-call-them deals.

Underwriting had always been the spigot that controlled an insurance company's bottom line. If a company needed more premium income, it might loosen the underwriting to let in more applicants. If there were too many death benefit payouts, a company would tighten its underwriting to keep out more of the riff-raff. Since potential SOLI/IOLI applicants had a particular, easy-to-identify profile—over 65 years of age with a high net worth and applying for high value policies—life insurance underwriters could keep a tight rein on applications that fit this profile. In some companies, underwriting had its collar buttoned down so tight it could hardly breathe. Barely anyone who fit the profile of a potential SOLI/IOLI candidate squeezed through, including many who didn't know a life settlement from Life Magazine. So why didn't these companies just classify every high net worth person over 65 as uninsurable? It certainly wasn't because of some ethical concern that they might be turning away many who had no intention of participating in a life settlement arrangement. Rather, if clearly insurable people were being denied insurance just because they fit a specific profile, it opened up the industry to all sorts of legal questions where ghastly words like discrimination and bias might get bandied about. And that was exactly the sort of publicity the life insurance industry—or any other industry for that matter—didn't need. So while many underwriters may have tightened the spigot on those who fit the life settlement profile, it wasn't usually turned off completely.

Instead, insurance companies came up with a trickier way to trip up SOLI/IOLI (or IILI or SPINLIFE or whatever-you-want-to-call-them) arrangements, and this way has become part and parcel to their current-day application process. In their life insurance applications, many insurance companies now ask questions like: "Has a life expectancy analysis (LE) ever been ordered on you?" or something similar. Because an LE is usually required at the beginning of the life settlement process, this question—when answered honestly—is designed to root out anyone who was acquiring insurance at the behest of a life settlement agent purely for the purpose of selling it to investors.

Another popular new question is: "Do you have any intention of selling this policy?"

A third crowd favorite: "Have you ever consulted a life settlement agent or provider?" or some variant thereof.

Obviously, any sort of "yes" answer to questions like these means the application will get an automatic, immediate thumbs down with no possibility for parole. Also, having a record of the applicant's responses to these questions enables the insurance company to create a file that can be used in future litigation if the company suspects a SOLI/IOLI transaction and wants to challenge a claim. What's truly interesting—and endlessly creative—are the varied and somewhat convoluted means some ... uh ... shall we say ... less than forthcoming life settlement agents have come up with to address these questions.

To meet the standards of the first question, some life settlement providers have begun to do life expectancy analysis in-house rather than shipping it out to LE companies. It means that if an applicant is asked if an LE has been ordered on them, they can now give an honest answer—"no." Will this hold up in a legal situation? Almost certainly. Does this, however, violate the spirit of the question? Almost certainly.

The second question—"Do you have any intention of selling this policy?"—often invokes a labyrinthine intellectual exercise in justification. What some life settlement agents will likely tell you here is that the day you fill out that application, you don't plan on selling that policy. Furthermore, they'll say that there is no way for you to know what you will want to do with the policy going forward. Whether or not you decide to sell it in two years or more is unknowable and therefore immaterial. Yeah, it's pretty tortured logic, but it's fairly solid in a legal sense. "Intent" has always been a lawyer's nightmare as it is almost impossible to prove. So, will this question cause legal problems down the road if someone does go ahead and sell their policy? No, probably not. Is answering "no" to this question when you're already working with a life settlement agent ethical? No, probably not.

The third question—"Have you ever consulted a life settlement agent or provider?"—is a real doozy. The best case scenario is that the applicant hasn't. Maybe you've read this little book here and have decided that having a life insurance policy as an investment is a good thing. Maybe you made this decision on your own without the help of a life settlement professional. We hope so. That will make us feel warm and fuzzy inside. Other than that ... well, some life settlement agents will claim that what they do is sell insurance ... they only do life settlements on the side. That, see, means they're not *really* a life settlement agent. Understand? Neither do we. But it's been said that it's a fool who looks for logic in the chambers of the human heart. And if that human heart really, really wants to make lots of money (and what heart doesn't?), we suspect a person can convince themselves of just about anything.

What did these questions do for the insurance industry's legal position vis-à-vis the life settlement industry? It did make many court cases less about insurable interest—where the industry was losing too many cases—and more about whether or not a person committed fraud on their application when they answered these questions if they subsequently turned around and sold their policy. It was firmer legal ground for the insurance industry to stand on. It still wasn't exactly bedrock, especially given the burden of proving intent and the great amount of creative flair a person could engage in when defending their answers, but it was more solid underfoot than the legal quicksand of insurable interest.

One thing needs to be emphasized, though. No matter what some in the insurance industry will have you believe, no matter what some ill-informed people may say or write, the truth is that life settlements themselves do not violate established insurance law in any way. This legal precedent has been concretely established by legal decision after legal decision. The legal target should be seeding techniques—strategies designed to get a person to buy a new insurance policy solely for the purpose of selling it right away. Non-recourse premium financing is the big kahuna here, of course. And even in these instances, the insurance application questions were designed to create a legal conflict where there really is none so that insurance companies have something more solid to go after when they attempt to deny a suspected SOLI/IOLI death benefit claim.

Perhaps the best way to look at this is to think about card counters working the blackjack table in a casino. There's nothing remotely illegal about card counting. There's nothing remotely unethical about card counting, either. It is amazing, though, to hear how many people think there is. Credit the casinos for creating this perception. The truth is, a card counter is simply someone who has found a legal way to exploit for their own benefit an existing system that is rigged against them. Nevertheless, casinos will do everything in their power from video surveillance to implementing complex face recognition computer software to smoke out those card counters so they can throw them out of the casino and blacklist them. Those card counters have found a way to game the system—a system which makes casinos loads and loads of money. Card counters take a little bite out of those massive profits, and for that, casinos will smite them with great vengeance and furious anger. The only crime those card counters ever committed was being too inconveniently clever for the casinos.

Now imagine that the casino is an insurance company; the card counter is a policyholder in a life settlement deal. Frankly, it all starts to come across as a little bit one-sided and unfair.

It should be pointed out that even after all of this, the insurance industry still only really managed to drag life settlements back into the legal gray area where they began. All of this creativity, all of this judicial energy, was expended by the insurance companies just to keep the legal question clearly ambiguous, a definite maybe, decidedly undecided. As you are reading this, there are probably lawyers somewhere in this country preparing this very moment to do battle yet again in yet another courtroom about yet another claim case that will debate all of these things yet one more time.

It occurred to some people in the life settlement industry that the best way to avoid all of this L.A. Law courtroom drama stuff would be to find some slick and sneaky way to prevent the insurance company from knowing that a policy's ownership had changed hands at all. If the insurance company could be kept in the dark, then it would just pay out the benefit with no risk of litigation and that would be that. It sounded like a perfectly devious plan. But what, oh what, to do?

Well, wouldn't you know it? Those clever little devils in the life settlement industry found just the thing …

The Trustfront Deal

Inspiration.

It's a whimsical beast.

One never knows from whence it will strike.

For non-recourse premium financing strategies, life settlement agents had once drawn inspiration from the fantastically uninspiring world of banking. For this latest little scheme, it was the estate planning realm that spawned a burst of nefarious creativity.

If life settlement agents could fix it so that ownership transfer of a policy could take place without the insurance company ever knowing about it, they could avoid lots of unpleasant things like the risk of litigation and legal challenges and angry giants swinging fists made of court orders and armies of lawyers armed with insurable interest laws.

Now, just as many people involved in life settlements were also banking people, many people involved in life settlements were also estate planning people. One of the most popular techniques used by wealthier estates during estate planning was the use of a *trust*.

For those who are unfamiliar with the term, a trust is a legal entity that can be assigned property ownership. A person—called the *grantor* or *settlor*—gives some type of property or asset to a person or organization—called the *trustee*—who is "trusted" to hold onto that property and take care of it for the benefit of a third person—a *beneficiary*. The grantor produces a *trust document* (sometimes also called a *trust instrument*) which legally binds the trustee to follow the exact letter of its instructions. Usually, this document describes in detail exactly how and under what conditions the beneficiary receives the property or assets in the trust. Legally, however, the trust remains the owner of the property until all of it has been distributed to the beneficiaries.

Trusts have been invaluable in estate planning for many years primarily because they just sort of happen to be excellent tax shelters. To put it very simply, assigning an estate to a trust upon death rather than directly to beneficiaries often enables that estate to effectively and legally dodge what can sometimes be very steep estate taxes.

While that's all well and good, that's not why life settlement providers were so hot on trusts. The real advantage from their perspective was that a trust could be granted ownership of an insured's policy, so instead of a person owning the policy, it would now be owned and administered by a trust. Yeah? So what? Well, if a trust owns the policy, it can change its beneficiary any time its administrator—the trustee—wants. Okay, great ... um ... so what? Well, a trustee can change the trust's beneficiary without the insurance company knowing a darn thing about it. Nothing is ever changed about the insurance policy itself. As far as the insurance company is concerned, the owner of the policy was, is and always shall be the trust. Same goes for the policy's beneficiary, which also was, is and always shall be the trust. Life settlements could now be conducted without the insurance company ever being the wiser. The trustee could simply change the terms of the trust without ever having to change the terms of the life insurance policy.

In these *trustfront deals*, investors were more or less undetectable by the insurance company. Not only could a provider receive a policy's death benefit without the insurance company knowing, it could also pay that policy's premiums invisibly. The provider simply funded the trust, then it was the trust that sent in premium payments.

The policy is then assigned to a trust. The trust is made the insurance policy's new beneficiary. The life settlor is the trust's grantor; the trustee is someone familiar to the agent or provider representative arranging the deal, though not someone who is directly associated with them. It can't be transparent to the insurance company that a trustfront deal is going on here, otherwise the game is up. Because trusts are used so often in estate planning techniques, the mere presence of a trust is not enough to ring any alarm bells, especially when used in conjunction with a high value policy. However, the presence of a trustee who is obviously connected to the agent or provider in some way would be a dead-to-rights tipoff. Now, the trust's beneficiary is set up to be the same as the original insurance policy's beneficiary for now. That way, any investigation into the trust at the outset shows everything to be above board and perfectly acceptable.

Sometimes, the usual two years pass to season the policy. Because of the level of invisibility granted to the investor in a trustfront deal, however, it is quite possible that providers will do a wet ink deal here. Regardless, the deal eventually goes down, and the provider is made the new beneficiary of the trust. When this happens, the life settlor is usually offered the return of any money spent on premiums, plus a small percentage of the face value of the policy as their cut for participating in the deal. Often, this percentage is

3%, though it can be more or less depending on the provider. Disturbingly often, providers have even been successful luring in new settlors with the comparatively paltry offer of a car or even just a little cruise. These settlors are rarely aware of just how much they *could* have gotten instead. Even the usual 3% piece of a relatively modest $1 million policy adds up to a $30,000 payoff. That's a whole lot more valuable than a cruise. And that's only on a $1 million policy.

The easiest way to illustrate how a trustfront life settlement deal works is to make our way through a real-world example …

Bill's Tale: A Case Study of a Trustfront Transaction

So there's this nice fellow named Bill. Bill is 76 years old and is as fit as a vegetarian, golf-playing fiddle. He's quite fond of money. He would like more of it around to keep him company. He is, however, a little impatient; he's the sort who repeatedly honks his car horn at red lights. He doesn't have any life insurance and doesn't really have any need for it, but he has heard of these life settlement arrangements and is interested in poking around to see what they're all about.

Bill wanders over to his insurance agent who happens to know a thing or two about life settlements. The agent tells Bill that he seems a good candidate and that he probably stands to make a nice chunk of change if he decides to take part in a life settlement transaction. It's also clear to the agent, however, that Bill is severely allergic to waiting. The agent suggests a trustfront life settlement. This means Bill will get his money upfront and without the two-year wait, then can virtually wash his hands of the whole affair thereafter. The agent informs Bill that he'll be willing to broker the deal as long as Bill understands that he'll have to fill out loads of paperwork, run out to get a medical exam, and temporarily foot the bill for the first year's premium, though it will be returned to him quickly. Bill's not especially keen on this last part, but he's been dealing with this agent for years and trusts him. He also really likes the idea of getting his money right away without having to wait two years for his payoff. So Bill signs on.

You see, people will do unusual things for money. They will rob banks. They will destroy old friendships. They will pause to pluck a quarter off the street while hurrying across a busy interstate highway. But as Woody Allen once said, "Money is better than poverty, if only for financial reasons." So when Bill is promised a lot of money essentially just to fill out paperwork and get a medical exam, it sure isn't hard to see why Bill goes for it, even with the risk of putting a full year's premium payment on the line.

The agent then gives Bill the usual exhausting stack of papers to fill out—a questionnaire including inquiries about his net worth, a health history questionnaire and a HIPAA form permitting a provider access to his private medical records. Then Bill goes home to watch Jeopardy. Meanwhile, the agent contacts the representative of a favorite provider. The representative, in turn, sets the wheels in motion for an in-house life expectancy analysis to be performed on Bill based on the information Bill gave and his medical records.

The agent now goes off in search of the best possible life insurance rate for Bill, meaning he's looking for a policy with the highest possible face value for the lowest possible premium cost given Bill's current insurance capacity. Bill's done well for himself and has a net worth in the neighborhood of $5 million. Bill's sharp golf game has kept him in good shape for his age, too. The agent is able to find Bill a quote for a $5 million preferred issue universal life policy with an annual premium of $245,000. Nice work, Secret Insurance Agent Man. The agent relays this information to the life settlement provider's representative.

Shortly thereafter, Bill gets a call … Good news! It looks like he's got the right stuff. The life settlement provider wants him onboard. The provider tables an offer: Bill will have to pay for the first year's premium on the policy but will be fully reimbursed for it when the policy transfer is made to the provider. Bill will also get 3% of the face value of the policy at that time. At that point, Bill will be free and clear. However, Bill must agree that he will answer some questions the provider might have from time to time thereafter—maybe once per year or so. These questions are designed to enable the provider to keep track of Bill's health, because if he suffers any problems, it will likely decrease his life expectancy and significantly increase the market value of his life insurance policy. Bill agrees.

An application is then filled out for the insurance. (And yes, poor Bill is subjected to the indignity of one of those dreaded medical exams.) On the application, Bill lists his son as the policy's sole beneficiary. The application is sent in. The whole process is for naught if the insurance company's underwriting turns down the application, so it's pins and needles time for everyone involved as they wait for word.

When word comes back, it's a happy day. Bill's application has been accepted; he has now joined the world of the insured. Birds sing, clouds dance, and the sun shines a bit brighter that day for all the characters in this tale.

Bill then pays the first annual premium for his new life insurance policy. As far as the insurance company is concerned, nothing fishy is going on here at all.

Next step. The agent sets up a trust. Bill serves as the trust's grantor; his policy is the property held in trust. For now, the beneficiary of the trust is the same as the beneficiary of the life insurance policy—namely, Bill's son. The trustee is some third-party individual or entity who the life settlement provider likes to use for exactly these situations. A trust document is produced instructing that any death benefit for Bill's policy should be paid in full to the trust's beneficiary.

Then … the trust is made the beneficiary of Bill's insurance policy. As mentioned before, this is not at all unusual in the life insurance industry as an estate planning move to avoid paying estate taxes. So from the insurance company's perspective, there's still nothing strange going on here. If the insurance company does in fact look into it a little deeper, all that it will find is that the trust's beneficiary is Bill's son—perfectly acceptable and still exactly like a typical tax-ducking estate planning strategy. Still nothing fishy.

From this point on, the trust is set up as the owner of the policy. Premium payments made for Bill's policy will come from the trust. The trust will be funded by the life settlement provider so that those premium payments can be made. In essence, the provider is paying for Bill's insurance; it's just doing it through the trust.

Now comes the big finale. The beneficiary of the trust is changed from Bill's son to the provider. As far as the insurance company knows, the trust pays for the policy, and the trust is still the policy's beneficiary. It has no idea that the trust has transferred its beneficial interest from Bill's son to an investor.

Once this transfer takes place, Bill gets reimbursed by the provider for that first year's premium, plus his reward of 3% of the face value of his $5 million policy—$150,000. With his part in this thing all done, Bill celebrates with a trip to New Zealand. We wish him the best of luck. It's a miserably long flight.

So now the ball stays in the life settlement provider's court. The provider keeps funding the trust, and the trust keeps paying the premiums on Bill's policy—$245,000 per year—like clockwork.

The life settlement provider now has a choice. It can hold onto Bill's policy and use it as its own investment, waiting for it to mature—meaning, the provider hangs onto it until Bill passes on so it can collect the death benefit. Or it can turn around and resell it again to another investor. Since the provider's outlay to this point has only been the $150,000 it gave Bill and the cost of the policy's premiums, it can still hope to make a significant profit by reselling the policy on the market.

The provider in our example opts for the second choice. But even with the trustfront protecting it from the watchful eyes of the insurance company, the provider still holds the policy for two years to let it season before making it available to the secondary market. One can never be too careful.

Two years pass …

There they go …

Now the life settlement provider calls Bill and updates their records on him to see if there have been any significant changes in his health. But no, Bill is still in great shape and playing a mean eighteen holes of golf, though the arthritis in his knee has been barking ever since that long flight to New Zealand. We told him so.

The provider makes Bill's policy available to the market and gets a bid from an investment firm for $1,300,000. Bill is now 78, but the most recent life expectancy analysis performed by the life settlement provider indicates that he should have at least six or seven more years in the tank. Rather than wait all that time (and maybe considerably longer) for the investment to mature, the provider agrees to the investment firm's offer.

Now … control of the trust is shifted to the investment firm. It now funds the trust to pay the policy's premiums, though the payments are still technically coming from the trust. The investment firm is now made the trust's beneficiary; the beneficiary of Bill's life insurance policy is still the trust.

That's just about it. The investment firm just keeps funding the trust to pay those premiums until Bill passes away. Let's say he did pass away rather suddenly just three years after the firm took control of his policy. As the beneficiary of the policy, the death benefit claim is filed on behalf of the trust, and the insurance company pays the death benefit payment to the trust. In accordance with the trust document, that death benefit is then paid out to the trust's beneficiary, which is the investment firm.

And that, friends, is the very end of this little tale.

We can now consult the financial scorecard to see how everyone did on the deal:

- Bill … well, he got $150,000 for selling something he got for free and didn't really want. He was a happy camper, indeed.

- The insurance agent who found Bill his high-value policy and referred him to the life settlement provider got half of the insurance sales commission—$110,500, in this case. Not too bad when you consider that Bill never would have bought life insurance without that life settlement deal to motivate him.

- The life settlement provider received the other half of the insurance sales commission—$110,500—plus the money it got when the investment bank bought the policy—$1,300,000. Its total costs were the money it paid to Bill—$150,000—plus the two years of premiums it paid while it was funding the trust—$245,000 per year for two years equaling a total cost of $490,000 in premiums. The provider's net profit? $770,500. Wow.

- And if you think that's good, wait till you see what the investment firm wound up with. Its net outlay was the $1,300,000 settlement it paid to the provider, plus the three years of premium payments—at a $245,000 annual premium, that adds up to $735,000 in total premium payments. That's $2,035,000 in costs. Steep, huh? Until you remember that the firm took in Bill's $5 million death benefit. Total profit to the firm: $2,965,000.

Holy Moses.

That's a lot of cash.

Granted, that figure is helped out a lot by Bill's early passing, but he would have to live quite a while past his projected life expectancy for there to be any real danger of the investment firm ever losing money on the transaction. If the firm continues to pay the $245,000 per year premiums, Bill would have to live beyond the age of 93, which is nearly nine years past his projected life expectancy. It's highly unlikely, but possible. But even if that were to happen, the investment firm almost certainly has a large pool of other policies, several of which will pay out earlier than life expectancy projections indicate. This will more than offset the lack of performance from those few that significantly outlive expectancies. So don't fret—those investors will make their money.

We could tell you were worried.

The Hybrid Horror

While standard non-recourse deals like the one we illustrated in chapter 6 and trustfront arrangements like the one we just went through here are both still very common in today's life settlement environment, a new life insurance industry horror is rearing its fearsome head.

Life settlement deals are being constructed now that combine the trickier elements of *both* non-recourse premium financing and trustfront schemes.

Even as the insurance companies are still working on their legal response to pure trustfront deals, arrangements have been emerging where a non-recourse loan is taken out by a trust or other legal entity (like an LLC) which uses the loan to finance the purchase of a new policy. In other instances, a non-recourse loan is used directly by a life settlement provider to fund a trust that is buying a policy. How this impacts the legal aspects of all this is unknown and undetermined for now. Rest assured that these arrangements will keep courtrooms buzzing well into the foreseeable future. What is certain is that these deals are becoming increasingly common.

What is also certain is that the growth in the secondary market is causing some ferocious competition among life settlement providers for the juiciest policies. Where once their only concern was slipping past the defenses of the life insurance companies, life settlement providers now find themselves battling each other quite fiercely in their eternal search for policies to buy.

This is excellent news for potential life settlors as it means that life settlement offers have improved to reflect this market-driven competition. Along with the evolution in settlement structure—like the combo non-recourse/trustfront deal—has come a comparable evolution in compensation structure. It is now common for an agent or a provider to offer a small amount of money upfront—say, 1% of the face value of a policy or some sort of flat fee—while still offering the settlor a portion of the life settlement deal down the road—maybe a full third of the settlement. In these situations, the settlor gets the best of both worlds—some money upfront and the more substantial payoff that can occur when they get a piece of the settlement.

If life insurance policies are biological real estate, it's clearly a seller's market out there.

Sounds pretty good, right? Time to jump on this ride and see where it goes. Whether it's a non-recourse premium financing deal or a trustfront transaction, you just want to pilot this ship right on out into the seas of instant prosperity …

But wait …

Before you start beating the bushes for the closest life settlement agent, let us present you with another option. We have a feeling that by the time we're done making our case, you won't want to do that non-recourse premium financing deal. You won't want to sign up for that trustfront settlement.

We have a better way.

Know how it's better?

Well, there are several reasons, really. One big one is that you won't have to enter into any arrangements of questionable legality or ethics. Another reason?

Money.

You'll make more of it our way. A whole heck of a lot more, in fact.

Interested?

We thought so.

Please let us explain …

8

Invest in Your Life: The Best Way to Invest in Your Life Insurance Policy

We want you to imagine something right now. It's a purely hypothetical, dreamtime vision, but suspend your disbelief for a moment here and let your mind wander with us a bit …

We want you to imagine a piece of property. It's awfully nice property. It sits on a beautiful, clear, mountain lake, except the water is always warm, and it only rains when you want it to. It's not a big piece of property, and it's undeveloped. No house, no marina, no seafood restaurant … nothing. Let's say this property—even undeveloped—is worth a cool $2 million on the real estate market.

Along comes a developer. It wants to build a marina complex, complete with jet ski and motor boat rental. Now in the past this developer has played a little fast and loose with the law. As a result, the developer is forbidden from buying property in the state where our beautiful mountain lake resides. And even if it could, the current property owner is a naturalist who has no intention of selling to someone who would muss up that pristine lake with icky, loud, polluting motor-boat-ish things.

This developer approaches you with a proposal. It asks that you buy that property for it, then transfer ownership to some other company that is affiliated with that developer but operates under a different name. This will conceal who is really buying that property both to the law and to the naturalist owner. The developer promises that you will be reimbursed for the property cost at the time of ownership transfer and will get a small fee in return for your trouble.

Would you do it?

No?

Okay, now what if, instead of a piece of land, it was a life insurance policy? Biological real estate instead of waterfront real estate.

Would you do it then?

We know that our little real estate scenario here lives in dreamland. We also know that it poses some different problems than those offered by a typical non-recourse premium financing life settlement or a trustfront deal. But legally, ethically, financially, it raises strikingly similar issues.

Problems with Those Non-Recourse Premium Financing Deals

There is no question that insurance companies don't like those non-recourse transactions; we went through why earlier in this book. There is also no question that insurance companies will continue to employ insurable interest laws on a state-by-state basis in an effort to kill those non-recourse deals stone dead. And insurance companies have gotten better at sniffing these sorts of arrangements out.

If an insurance company's underwriters detect one of these deals when you're first applying for insurance, your application will simply get turned down flat and that'll spell the end of it. However, you may find the insurance company may not look too kindly upon any future insurance applications you send in. You just might've burned that bridge down to the ground.

If, however, your insurance company figures out that your policy has been financed by a non-recourse transaction after it's already in force, you're not going to go to jail. You're not going to lose your house. But the insurance company will almost certainly rescind your policy. If that does happen, it will often occur within the first two years your policy is in force—the dreaded contestable period—so there's not a whole lot you could do to fight back.

But what does having your policy rescinded really mean if you acquired that policy through a non-recourse financed life settlement arrangement? The non-recourse nature of the loan protects your assets from being attacked by the lender if the deal falls through. In some cases, though, you might have had to pay a small upfront fee to initiate the transaction. That money could be gone. Not to mention all the time and effort that went into setting up the deal. All those annoying forms you filled out and those trips to the agent were for a whole lot of nothing.

Worse, however, is that while this deal fell to pieces, you just happened to get older. That's a good thing. Or at least it's better than the alternative. But if you're trying to get your hands on some new life insurance, older isn't better. In fact, getting older can be a deal-breaker once you've wandered into the golden years. If a year or two passed, you can now fully expect it to be harder to find a company that will offer you life insurance. If you do find one, that insurance will be more expensive. So, in a sense, having your policy rescinded actually did cost you money. Plus, it's possible that over the course of that time, you developed some health conditions that will make it even more difficult or expensive to get new life insurance, if it's possible at all.

And let's face it, when an insurance company catches you trying to outsmart them by dancing around their regulations, you didn't make any friends there. Instead, you probably just landed yourself on a list of red-flagged troublemakers. So if and when you do send in that new application for insurance, you probably shouldn't bother sending it to the company whose sensibilities you just offended. The reception could be chillier than a penguin's tuckus.

And if these reasons aren't enough to convince you to avoid non-recourse deals, there's another real whopper: *phantom income*. There are some what-ifs that need to fall exactly the wrong way for this to turn around and bite you. Still, it pays to know just what can happen in a worst-case scenario.

Let's say you used a non-recourse transaction to get yourself a $10 million policy. Now let's say the premiums on this policy are about $500,000 per year. The non-recourse loan necessary to pay for two years of coverage is $1 million, plus interest. Now imagine that the insurance company did some digging and found out that this was a non-recourse deal. It rescinds the policy right on the cusp of two years of in force coverage. Obviously, this shatters the deal, and that's the end of it. The non-recourse lender can't go after any of your other assets, so you're more or less in the clear there. The loan collateral—the rescinded policy—is gone, and the lender cannot recoup that money. For all intents and purposes, the lender just paid for two years of your life insurance without getting anything back. Fine. No skin off your teeth.

Here's the problem … In an instance like this, the lender will usually send a 1099 statement to you for the amount of debt that went unpaid. The government calls this *forgiveness of debt income*. That's right … it's called income even if you never actually got a penny of that money yourself. That's why we prefer to call it phantom income. And what does every good little citizen have to do when he or she gets income? That's right … we pay taxes on it. And you know what that means … yep, you got it—you might end up paying taxes on the loan you took out as if you earned it as income. Somewhere in the world, there may be something more annoying than paying income tax on money you never got. If so, we hope to never experience it.

We could also launch into a harangue about ethics right about here—that's what the insurance industry has done as part of its media campaign—but we're not sure how appropriate that is. Ethics are a personal thing. If a person wants something badly enough, they will gently reshape their ethics in such a way as to render that something permissible. Furthermore, many, many people engaged in non-recourse premium financing deals without even the slightest clue that what they were doing was objectionable to the insurance community. These folks had no idea that the legality and the ethics of the transaction had been called into question. And when they wound up rather suddenly and perhaps even a little unexpectedly actually getting those two "free" years of life insurance and a big chunk of money, they could hardly be blamed for spreading the word to family and friends. So we'll leave answering those ethical questions up to you.

But what if we told you that the worst thing that could happen to you in a non-recourse premium financing life settlement is for it to go perfectly?

See, if everything progresses exactly as the life settlement agent or provider planned, if the whole deal goes point for point as it would be written in the life settlement textbook if such a thing existed, if it all runs absolutely, indisputably flawlessly ... you lose.

How?

Because even though you would end up with a nice pile of money, you or your family/beneficiaries could have done much better.

More on that in just a moment.

In the meantime, let's take a quick look at ...

Problems with Those Trustfront Deals

Many of the potential problems with trustfront arrangements are pretty similar to those you might face in a non-recourse transaction. But the proliferation of trustfront deals is a newer phenomenon, and it remains problematic for companies to differentiate between trustfront deals and those involving traditional estate planning techniques. The insurance industry's legal resistance against trustfront deals doesn't seem to have organized to the level of that against non-recourse transactions. Eventually, it will.

Trustfront schemes are even shakier from a legal perspective than non-recourse deals, and they present a different sort of financial risk to the settlor. An advantage of trustfront transactions is that many often involve the settlor receiving upfront money rather than having to wait two years. If this is the case, it takes one element of personal risk out of the equation. The price for that, though, is that the settlor must usually pay for that first premium. If that money comes out of the settlor's pocket, then there clearly is a new risk. If anything goes wrong—the deal falls through, the settlement provider goes out of business or is a fraud—the settlor will lose that premium money. If the settlor happened to finance that payment with an illegal bridge loan ... well, it's an illegal bridge loan. And that could lead to no end of hard core legal trouble.

But just like a non-recourse deal, the real problem with a trustfront transaction is if the whole thing runs impeccably. Because if it does, if you wind up getting that chunk of upfront cash exactly as planned, you just lost money. And a lot of it, too. There's really no nice way of putting it …

Non-recourse premium financing transactions offer a poor return on your life insurance policy. And if the return off a non-recourse transaction is bad, the usual trustfront deal's return is downright Lousy with a capital "L."

Wanna know what's better?

The Right Way to Invest In Your Life

Okay, let's just forget about the legal ambiguities surrounding non-recourse and trustfront schemes for a second. Let's set aside the ethical questions, the risks, the potential for phantom income … all that stuff. We know you're a loyal listener of WIIFM—What's In It For Me radio. So let's get down to brass tacks …

You want to make the most money you can off your policy. We think that's a pretty safe statement. You either have an asset or want to acquire an asset—a life insurance policy—and you want to get the best return possible for the sale of the asset or you would like to get the maximum value or "rate of return on premiums paid" to your family if you or your trust hold the policy until your death. If you didn't care about your return, if you weren't concerned about maximizing your life settlement potential, you wouldn't have picked up the book you've got in your hands right now.

As troublesome as legal, ethical or risk-factor questions may be in regard to non-recourse or trustfront life settlements, the biggest problem with them is that they waste a large portion of your policy's earning power. How? By funneling that money away from you—the settlor—and toward the other parties involved in the transaction.

So how do we fix this? How do we get more money into the pockets of settlors rather than into the coffers of lenders, providers and middlemen?

The solution is impossibly simple …

You begin by buying your own policy. No non-recourse loans. No illusionary money. You put a little skin in the game, a little cash on the barrelhead, and you'd be amazed at how much more agreeable those insurance companies will be. Especially, now that we are exploring the possibility that this policy may be sold on the secondary market. This is really what we call a "wait and see" approach. The reality is that many people with the assets necessary to qualify for these policies may become very comfortable with the idea of controlling their own life insurance asset. They will be willing to wait for a period of time (2,3,5,10 years) until they make a decision about selling or keeping the policy. The longer the policy is held, the more they become informed about its ultimate value on the secondary market. This helps in the decision to keep or sell the policy.

All the insurance companies really want is the assurance that you just might hang onto your policy rather than the certainty that you're going to sell it. If you pay for your policy with a non-recourse loan, the company knows you don't have any intention of holding that policy for any longer than necessary before pawning it off. Sure, it's possible to keep a policy even in a non-recourse deal, but the entire transaction is structured to facilitate the sale and discourage holding the policy. First, the deal has been set up by a life settlement agent or provider, That signals quite clearly that the intent is to sell the policy from the get-go. Also, because it's been set up by someone who stands to profit from the transaction, there may be hidden penalties or costs for backing out of the deal. But even if there are no sneaky, little penalties, holding the policy will still cost you money, because you will have to cover the high interest when you pay off the non-recourse loan. And that additional cost is a potent discouraging factor when considering whether or not to hold the policy.

Now if you pay for that policy yourself instead and acquire it without entering into any sort of contract with a life settlement agent or provider, there is a chance for the old "puppy dog close," one of the most effective techniques in sales.

The puppy dog close works like this: If a family with several children decides that they may or may not want a dog, they might go to a shelter to look at a few pups. The shelter may then allow them to keep one of the puppies for a few days to see if they want it. Once the dog has stayed with the family and they've given it a cute name like Muffin or Beans, what do you suppose the chances are that Mom and Dad are going to ignore the tearful protests of the children and barbarously drag poor little Beans back to the shelter? Pretty small, we'll wager. Basically, the puppy dog close is a metaphor for the sales concept of "try before you buy." The notion is that if a person tries a product, they will see its value and want to keep it.

This is something the insurance companies can get behind. What they want is for you to buy your policy, then hold onto it for a while. The thinking is that many policyholders will see the value in life insurance during this time and decide to keep it rather than send it back to the shelter. After two years, you can control (either by paying the premiums out of pocket or by employing some of the traditional "insurance company friendly" financing techniques) a very substantial life insurance asset.

As we have discussed throughout this book, life insurance is now an asset class that Wall Street is embracing. This is causing a "trickle down effect" that allows us now to teach individuals how to become involved in owning life insurance as an asset. By owning the policy yourself, you leave yourself with the following attractive options:

1. **<u>Hold the Policy Until Your Death</u>** –

    ▪ Now this may not be what you were expecting us to say. We have talked a lot about the secondary market and life settlements, but holding a life insurance policy until death is a fundamental "Invest in Your Life" strategy. It has the potential to provide the highest rate of return. This rate of return is to your family, charity, or other beneficiary– not to you because for this option only comes into play upon your death. Many clients, however, see this as the most natural and effective strategy with this asset. Since they have worked a lifetime to accumulate and protect their estate and are passing it to their beneficiaries, why not continue with their life insurance asset. One of the most interesting parts of this strategy comes down to the actual rate of return on investment when you compare the total premiums paid to the ultimate death benefit of the policy. Historically, when we look at these rates of return, we have been able to show clients the following type of returns (please note that these are based upon a 75 year old female, in good health, with an A+ rated insurance company):

Year	Rate of Return On Death Benefit
10	21.55%
13*	13.07
15	9.71
20	4.83

    *Empirical Life Expectancy

    ▪ When you consider that these rates of return are based upon a tax-free death benefit, these are compelling numbers as a long term investment. They become more compelling when you consider the possibility of an adverse change in health of the insured after the policy is issued. This occurrence would drop the life expectancy number and make the expected rate of return on death benefit even higher.

2.   <u>Settle the Policy on the Secondary Market</u>

- The fact that you have bought the policy yourself and have owned it for a period of time (2,3,5,10 years) gives you a legitimate option to see what the value of your policy is on the secondary market. The value of this type of policy, all else being equal, will be among the most valuable on the market – and here is why – it is very "clean" paper and that is what investors will pay top dollar for. It is very clean because there is no unusual financing arrangement (non-recourse or the like) and no "trustfront" arrangement. When this type of policy goes to the secondary market, there will be the most investors interested in the paper, which can drive up the price substantially. This is the position in which any seller would like to be. There will be a lot more information in this and other chapters on life settlements. We want to make it clear that this is only *one* of the options that you have when you employ the Invest in Your Life strategy.

3.   <u>Utilize one of the Many Option the Insurance Company Will Offer</u>

- As the life insurance companies get familiar with the secondary market, they have already begun to create interesting policy options, within their own systems, to "combat" offers on the secondary market. These options will include accelerated death benefits, interest free loans, and other choices designed to entice the policy owner to retain the policy rather then settle it on the secondary market.

The key is that you must own and control the policy to take advantage of any of the options listed above. It's sort of like the lottery – "you gotta be in it to win it!"

If you have the ready cash to afford it, the money for a policy's premiums ideally ought to come out of your own pocket. You know, just as if you were buying insurance like a regular life insurance customer. Because, in fact, you *are* a regular life insurance customer. No tricks. No schemes. You're just another life insurance policyholder paying for their premiums like anyone else.

If you don't have the liquidity to pay for the life insurance premiums for a high-value policy, there are far more traditional financing options available than a non-recourse loan. We'll get into that a little bit later in this chapter. While the best way to maximize profitability is to pay those premiums without a loan, financing a life insurance policy through traditional means can make sense in certain circumstances.

The bottom line is that you now have complete control of your own policy. Hopefully, you don't owe anything to any lender at this point. If you did borrow, the terms of the loan are fully under your control, and you undoubtedly got a much better interest rate than you would have gotten through a non-recourse loan.

The next step is just to hang onto that policy. Obviously, the minimum amount of time to hold your policy is two years so that you can season it past the contestability period. However, selling your policy the very day it turns two years old may raise some concerns at the insurance company. It may cause them to suspect that your policy was the object of a SOLI/IOLI transaction from the beginning, and that will mean a potential *file audit*. This means that company officials will pore through the records looking for holes, weaknesses, inconsistencies, or general excuses to claim fraud and kill the policy. If everything in your application and insurance company dealings has been 100% above board and honest, they won't find anything constituting fraud that could serve as legal justification for rescinding the policy. But it is a reasonable assumption that the company will err on the side of caution and threaten to rescind if there are any real questions.

Another choice would be to hold that policy for longer than the two-year minimum. Patience is a virtue and all that. If you enter into this thing with the notion of this being a three- or even a four-year investment, you won't get impatient and risk pulling the trigger early enough to arouse the ire of the insurance company. Now, holding the policy will cost more money in premiums, but each year you get older, your policy gains value as your projected life expectancy grows shorter. It is even quite possible that your policy gains more value over that extra time than you end up spending in additional premiums, especially if you are unfortunate enough to have been diagnosed with any new health conditions during that period.

When you're ready to sell your policy, it's time to approach a life settlement professional. You have two options here. You can go to a life settlement agent or broker, or you could go straight to the life settlement providers themselves. Each has its own advantage.

If you choose to go with a broker or an agent, you will be taking some of the legwork out of the process for yourself. Basically, what you're hiring is a comparison shopper; the agent or broker will contact a number of different life settlement providers to find the best offer for your policy. But this service is hardly free. The agent may take as much as a third of the life settlement— maybe even more—to perform this little service for you. Still, it does simplify the procedure greatly from your end. Our advice is to interview some reputable settlement brokers and choose carefully with whom you choose to work. Also, we suggest that there is almost always room to negotiate with the agent on his or her fee. In almost all situations, one third is a substantial fee. If you negotiate, you should be able to arrive at something more reasonable like 20%.

And there it is … The super-secret, super-effective, super-legal way to make money with your life insurance policy. It's not rocket science. In fact, it's about as simple as it gets. Buy a policy, hold it, sell it yourself. Simple as pie on a stick. Don't give your money away to middlemen, and don't be swayed by come-ons from life settlement agents or providers offering you anything less than the entirety of your life settlement.

It's your policy. Shouldn't you be the one making the most money off it?

Case Study Comparison: Invest in Your Life Versus Non-Recourse Premium Financing

Maybe you remember Roger. He's our vodka-martini swilling, sailboat-owning pinochle wizard from chapter 6 who participated in one of those non-recourse premium financing deals. Let's reiterate the bare details of that transaction once again just to refresh your memory.

Roger is 74 years old and gets a standard $5 million universal life policy with an annual premium of $225,000. He works with an agent who contacts a provider for him and sets up a non-recourse loan with an 18.7% interest rate to pay for two years of premiums. After holding for two years, Roger sells the policy to a hedge fund manager who serves as this life settlement's provider. The provider offers $1,045,000 for the policy. The complete financial results of this transaction can be found in chapter 6. But here, let's focus in on a few specific aspects of this little deal:

- The non-recourse lender earned an awfully fat profit from the high-interest loan—$184,036. And all that profit was earned on what was only a two-year loan.

- The life settlement agent got one-third of the life settlement profit after the non-recourse loan had been paid off. That added up to $153,667.

- Roger got the remaining two-thirds of the settlement profit—$307,333.

Roger sure seems to have done pretty well; $307,333 is nothing to thumb your nose at, is it? But a quick examination here shows just how much of his policy's value he gave away. If he had done a life settlement without a non-recourse loan, he wouldn't have had to pay $184,036 worth of high interest payments. Also, he lost a full third of his post-loan profits by going through an agent rather than taking it to a provider himself. What if he had bought that policy and treated it like a traditional short-term real estate investment for two years, then turned around and sold it on the market himself? Here's how that would have looked:

- Obviously, there'd be no non-recourse lender to pay off. That's $184,036 saved.

- He takes our advice and negotiates a 20% fee instead of the usual one third. Another $69,150 in the kitty for Roger.

- So how much better could Roger have done by Investing in His Life rather than through a non-recourse deal? He would've received the settlement for $1,045,000. Take from that the cost of two years' worth of premiums that he would have paid out of pocket and the negotiated settlement fee; you get a two year profit to Roger of $502,800. In the non-recourse scenario, Roger only made out with $307,333. To put this in perspective, investing in this simple buy-and-hold strategy versus going through a non-recourse arrangement earned Roger a staggering $195,467 extra, yielding a 64% increase in final profit.

So how does earning a few hundred thousand grand more sound? Not too tough to take, right? And it was all done nice and legal-like.

All this simple strategy does is channel all the money to where it should go—to you as the settlor—rather than to other parties. In a typical non-recourse arrangement, the lender does well. So does the agent. But all at the settlor's expense.

And if you think this is a convincing case against non-recourse premium financing deals, wait till you how much you lose in a typical trustfront ...

Case Study Comparison: Invest in Your Life Versus Trustfront Deals

Impatient Bill, 76 year-old vegetarian and golfer, was our trustfront participant from chapter 7. He just couldn't bear the thought of hanging in there for a whole two years waiting for his investment to mature. He had to get his hands on his money upfront and nothing else would do. His agent was happy to oblige and set him up with an upfront-paying trustfront settlement.

The policy the agent was able to secure for Bill was a $5 million preferred issue universal life policy with an annual premium of $245,000. Bill agreed to a deal where he would get 3% of the $5 million face value of his policy, or $150,000, right upfront. It's a typical payment for a deal of this nature, though payments of considerably less—maybe 1% or 2%—are also common. It's also a sadly frequent occurrence that a trustfront life settlor would actually only receive a car or cruise or some other fixed asset "prize" for acquiring and selling a life insurance policy. Yuck. Please … if you remember nothing else from this book, remember this … Do **not** sell away your policy for a car or a cruise. It's worth **so much more** than that.

So the provider found by Bill's agent purchases the policy from him for a mere $150,000. It is then this provider that turns around and sells the policy to the end investor—an investment firm who pays the provider $1,300,000. In this case, that first provider who bought Bill's policy functions as nothing more than a middleman; the real provider in this example is the investment firm who paid the $1,300,000 for the life settlement.

Our math skills may be a little fuzzy, but even we're pretty sure that $1,300,000 is a bit more than $150,000. Sure, it initially looked like Bill did quite nicely by walking away with $150,000. But when you consider how much more he *didn't* walk away with … It kinda looks like Bill got the ugly end of this deal.

What if Bill had used the Invest in Your Life strategy and had bought the policy himself—no tricky trustfront necessary, thank you very much—had held onto it for two years, then had sold directly to the secondary market? He would have dealt directly with the investment firm provider; there would have been no other provider serving as a middleman. How would that change things? Oh, just a little …

- In Bill's trustfront deal, he got $150,000 upfront.

- The life settlement provider middleman, however, did a wee bit better. It paid Bill $150,000 for the policy and paid for two years of premiums before reselling the policy. At $245,000 per year, that's an additional $490,000 in premium costs for a total outlay of $640,000. Meanwhile, the middleman provider took in $1,300,000 from the settlement. Total profit to the middleman: $660,000.

Now, if Bill had acquired and sold this policy himself:

- He took our advice and negotiated a 20% fee with the life settlement agent.

- The result? Bill gets his own policy and pays two years of premiums for a cost of $490,000. He approaches life settlement providers directly and gets 80% of the $1,300,000 or $1,040,000. Total profit to Bill: $550,000.

By going through a middleman, by settling for a 3% upfront payment, by not doing this the right way, Bill threw an extra $400,000 out the window.

Ouch. Double ouch, actually.

Maybe some people can afford to toss almost one-half a million bucks in the river. But we can't imagine why they'd want to.

Invest in Your Life Versus the Hybrid Deal

Let's examine one more case.

Let's take a look at the rising new wave of seeding techniques—the dreaded multi-headed hydra of the non-recourse/trustfront hybrid. In these deals, it's quite common for the settlor to receive a combination of an upfront payment—like you might see in a trustfront case—with a portion of the final life settlement—like you would see in a non-recourse transaction. We're going to be generous here and present you with the most favorable terms you are likely to see in any of these new generation arrangements and compare that with the simple Invest in Your Life strategy.

Let's look at our buddy Roger, our non-recourse case, again. His policy was worth $5 million with that $225,000 annual premium, and it was financed with a two-year 18.7% interest non-recourse loan. Roger was offered a life settlement worth $1,045,000 on that policy. In a very generous hybrid deal given his policy and life expectancy, Roger might get 1% of the face value of that policy upfront, with a full two-thirds of the final settlement profit. He wouldn't have to pay any money out-of-pocket; the non-recourse loan would take care of all his premium payments. On the contrary, Roger would get upfront money just for signing on with the deal. Sounds like this offspring got the best genes from both the non-recourse and trustfront sides of the family. And with a rich compensation rate that's a bear to find out there in the real world to boot. Looks like the perfect deal ...

Until you compare it to the Invest in Your Life solution.

In the hybrid deal, Roger would score 1% of the policy's face value as soon as the life settlement transaction was approved and signed, yielding an upfront payment of $50,000. With the non-recourse loan handling the premiums, he'd have no cash outlay. but the interest on that loan (and the premium costs themselves, of course) will be taken out of the $1,045,000 life settlement. To put it simply, Roger would get exactly what he would get with the non-recourse case study outlined previously, plus $50,000 for the upfront "sweetener." The end result is that after two years Roger earns $357,333.

Compare that to the Invest in Your Life strategy's two-year bottom line: a profit of $502,800.

Which strategy looks better to you?

Unless, of course, you really hate the notion of earning an additional $145,517. Because if you're terribly stressed out about how you're going to spend that cash, you'd be better off doing it their way. Then you won't have all that inconvenient extra money to worry about.

Traditional Premium Financing

In some cases, it might pay to finance premium payments with a traditional loan. You may find that you want to get a policy with a higher face value than your current liquidity can support, so a loan might make sense to help pay for the premiums. We'd advise proceeding carefully here, though. It's obviously a simpler deal to only purchase a policy with a face value for which you can afford to pay the premiums out of pocket. A loan may enable you to acquire a policy with a higher value, thereby significantly increasing its investment value both for any beneficiaries you might want to cover and for yourself when you sell it to the secondary market. However, that loan accrues interest costs, reducing the net return on your investment. The interest costs could negate all the investment return gains you made by bumping up the policy's face value in the first place.

It should be stated, however, that the interest rates for a loan to finance a life insurance policy tend to be very affordable, especially if you express your willingness to participate in a life settlement to the lender. A common rate for a traditional premium financing loan will be along the lines of LIBOR + 2%, resulting in a typical APR in the neighborhood of 7–9%. Compare that bargain rate to the astronomical APRs typical of non-recourse premium financing loans—somewhere around 15–19%—and there isn't much doubt as to which provides the stronger investment return.

The cost for that much lower interest rate is the commitment of collateral. In non-recourse premium financing, the policy itself is the only collateral, so there's no money or property on the line for the settlor—no skin in the game. As we've mentioned numerous times before, insurance companies just hate this. In a traditional premium financing loan, the settlor puts some property at stake in order to take out a *collateral loan*. If he or she should default on the loan, the lender would take control of the collateral and sell it to pay for the loan cost. Insurance companies are far more agreeable to traditional premium financing solutions where the insured has some real equity at stake in the policy. And collateral loans always get much more favorable interest rates from lenders because of the guarantee of return.

Furthermore, lenders in these situations rarely demand a one-for-one valuation match between collateral and loan, especially if the prospective insured indicates their willingness to participate in a life settlement. In other words, if you want to pay for two years' worth of premium payments when you have an annual premium of $250,000, you usually won't have to put up $500,000 worth of collateral. Lending institutions are investors themselves (and often potential life settlement providers), so they know the value of a life insurance policy in today's secondary market. They are fully aware that lending to someone willing to participate in a life settlement is hardly a risk at all. If the borrower ever really needs to pay off that loan, all he or she would have to do is sell the policy, and that loan can be paid off. As a result, the collateral demands are small, and the loan's interest rate is low and highly affordable.

All of this notwithstanding, it's still a much better deal to avoid borrowing that money unless you have a darn good reason. Why pay the interest rates for any loan if it is avoidable? Still, in cases where liquidity might only be an immediate, short-term problem, a person might consider taking out a traditional premium financing loan. This loan could then be paid back as soon as the policy is sold in a life settlement or if money becomes available for any other reason. A person might also consider a premium financing loan if a great majority of their personal worth is tied up in fixed assets like real estate or art pieces. This person may have a great personal net worth and so could normally acquire a high-value life insurance policy, but may not have much worth immediately accessible in liquid cash. Paying the premiums might therefore be a strain, so a loan could be used as a temporary source of ready money. As with any loan, though, the goal should always be to pay it off as soon as possible to help boost the value of the policy's investment return.

Let's look at our test case studies again. This time, we'll compare the returns of our non-recourse/trustfront/hybrid deals with an Invest in Your Life solution that has been financed by a traditional premium financing loan.

Traditional Premium Financing Case Study Comparison

First contender up is Roger with his non-recourse premium financing transaction …

For his $5 million policy with its $225,000 annual premium, Roger was set up with a two-year 18.7% interest non-recourse loan. He received a life settlement worth $1,045,000 on that policy.

Roger's net profit using non-recourse premium financing: $307,333.

Let's say Roger financed two years of premiums with a traditional premium financing solution, resulting in a $450,000 loan with an interest rate at LIBOR + 2%. At the time of this transaction, this produced a total interest cost of $61,133.

Roger's net profit with the Invest in Your Life strategy: $502,800.

The winner: Invest in Your Life, by a $189,467 knockout.

Next contender, Bill and his trustfront deal …

Bill got a $5 million policy with an annual premium of $245,000. He agreed to a deal where he would get 3% of the policy's face value upfront as his payment. The life settlement value of the policy was $1.3 million.

Bill's net profit: obviously, just the $150,000 upfront payment.

Now imagine if Bill had financed two years of premiums with traditional premium financing. This resulted in a $490,000 loan taken out with an interest rate at LIBOR + 2%. At the time of this transaction, this produced a total interest cost of $73,836.

Bill's net profit with the Invest in Your Life strategy: $476,164.

The winner in a one-sided mismatch: Invest in Your Life, by a first-round $326,164 slaughter.

Final contender, Roger again, but this time with a hybrid deal …

Roger had a $5 million policy with a $225,000 annual premium, which was purchased with a two-year 18.7% interest non-recourse loan. As a sweetener, he received 1% of the policy's face value upfront when he signed on for the deal. Two years later, he got two-thirds of the life settlement, which was worth $1,045,000.

Roger's net profit with the hybrid deal: $357,333.

Had Roger financed two years of premiums with a traditional premium financing solution, it would have resulted in a $450,000 loan with an interest rate at LIBOR + 2%. At the time of this transaction, this would have produced a total interest cost of $61,133.

Roger's net profit with the Invest in Your Life strategy: $441,667.

The winner: Invest in Your Life, by a convincing $84,334 decision. In any of these cases, should the insured have chosen to hold the policy until their death, the clear winner would be their beneficiaries. Again, the winner – Invest in Your Life, by potentially millions of dollars.

Looks like we have a champion.

We're so proud.

A Quick Look at Policy Splitting

Apart from the obvious monetary benefit—not to mention all the legal advantages—the Invest in Your Life strategy gives you complete control over the terms of your life settlement. Always remember that providers are desperate for your policy. This is a seller's market in a big way. Each provider you contact is auditioning for you, not the other way around. If you fit the profile of a typical life settlement candidate and you're looking for a provider to buy your policy, there's an excellent chance you'll find more than one. Feel free to not only comparison shop, but also to negotiate any terms that may be beneficial to you. If you have a desirable policy, you'll be holding fistfuls of negotiating power.

One nice little perk you might want to look into is the possibility of *policy splitting*. This enables you to sell part of your policy to a life settlement provider, while keeping the rest for traditional life insurance purposes. This can be particularly useful for someone who has had a life insurance policy for a long time, but no longer needs all that insurance coverage. Rather than sell away all of the policy, the holder could sell part of it to a provider and keep the rest for his or her beneficiaries. Many providers offer this as an option, so be sure to bring it up with them when you're negotiating the terms of your settlement if it's something that interests you.

9

Step by Step: The Invest in Your Life Process

While the Invest in Your Life process is a simple one, there are a several tips and tidbits you'll want to keep in mind when using a life insurance policy as an investment. These considerations change depending on your age, whether or not you currently have a policy, and the type of policy you have if you have one, so we're going to divide our recommendations up into six separate categories, each of which addresses a particular set of conditions *(As always, we encourage you to look at the value of holding your policies until death. This will provide the greatest investment value and rate of return to your beneficiary)*:

- someone 65 or older with an active permanent policy

- someone 65 or older with an active term policy

- someone 65 or older without a policy

- someone under 65 with an active permanent policy

- someone under 65 with an active term policy

- someone under 65 without a policy

In just a few minutes, you can read through a lot of the things it took us six years to learn in this crazy business of ours …

Someone 65 or Older with an Active Permanent Policy

If you're in this group, you are the sweet spot, the wheelhouse, the engine that drives the life settlement industry. You have the most straightforward path to investment, and you offer what providers and investors most want to work with, especially if you're over 70 years of age. 65 is acceptable but still a bit too young to be ideal. At that age, you might have some trouble finding providers willing to buy the policy. Even if you do, the policy valuation will not be as high as you might like. On the other hand, isn't it nice to still be too young for something at the age of 65?

There's always a bright side ...

Someone 65 or Older with an Active Term Policy

Policyholders in this situation might find themselves in something of a windfall scenario. Most policyholders of term insurance count on eventually lapsing their coverage and never even consider the notion that their policy might be worth something as an investment. Most also assume that all those premium payments were thrown into a big, yawning, black hole from which no return on that money will ever emerge. The truth is that a term policy is a personal asset; it has investment value. But to tap into that value, a policyholder might have to take an extra step or two that permanent life insurance policyholders don't have to go through.

You may find, however, that some investors will buy your term insurance policy without any additional steps. This is more likely if you're of an advanced age (at least 75 years old, preferably older) and have a high-value, longer term policy that isn't going to expire for several more years. Of course, this particular set of circumstances is pretty unlikely; most insurance companies won't make term coverage available to older policyholders, and high-value term policies for longer-term coverage are particularly rare for older insurance-seekers. But if you do meet these criteria and have a life expectancy that falls within the remaining time left on your term, investors may take a chance and gamble on your term policy.

Still, most providers and investors aren't particularly interested in buying term insurance. As described earlier in this book, term insurance is life insurance with an expiration date, and life insurance with an expiration date isn't a very good investment. But dress that term insurance up by converting it to permanent insurance and suddenly you're the belle at the ball. Just like that, you've got yourself a highly desirable commodity the market will pay well for. And all it really takes is a little policy conversion paint job.

So for a term policyholder, the first step in evaluating your investment options is always finding out whether your term policy is convertible. Most—but not all—term policies are. In your policy's documentation, look for a section called "Right to Convert" or something similar. The terms for conversion will be outlined there. If you don't find that section or you need further clarification, you can always contact your insurance company.

If your policy is not convertible, you can still go through the pricing process to see if it's worth something. If you have been diagnosed with a life-threatening condition or are at least 75 years of age or older, there may be takers in the market, especially if your policy's term lasts for more than one year.

If your policy is convertible, you have two options: go through the entire policy pricing process for the term policy or convert it first. Really, there is no harm in gauging your current term policy's price before conversion. While pricing for that, you might want to ask brokers and providers how the offers and terms would change if it were a permanent policy instead. But if you're approaching providers yourself, it's a time-consuming process. You may find that there is no interest in your term policy at all. If this is the case, you may decide to convert before wasting a lot of time and effort pricing a term policy no one really wants.

If and when you decide to convert, there are a few pieces of information you should carry with you into the conversion process:

- **Most term policy conversions do not require a new medical exam.** We're sure you're saddened by this.

- **Many term policies are issued with a classification guarantee that enables you to convert to a permanent policy at the same health risk classification as your term policy.** If your health has taken a downward turn since you first got that term policy, you can still maintain your more favorable health classification when you convert without being underwritten at a lower, more expensive risk class.

- **On the other hand, if your health has improved since you first got your term insurance, you might want to go through medical underwriting again.** You could get bumped up to a more favorable risk class and save lots of money in premium cost. Now that's worth a trip to the ole' doctor, isn't it?

- **You can only convert to a permanent policy with the same insurance company.** There's no switching teams in the middle of the game.

- **You may be limited as to which permanent plans you can convert to.** Because you are doing this for investment reasons, it is highly recommended that you convert to the type of policy that most investors are looking for—namely, universal life. If that isn't an option, whole life will do, but universal life will draw investors like a trout fillet draws cats.

- **Because you plan on selling the policy, cash value isn't a concern.** If offered a choice between plans, choose one that maximizes face value while minimizing premium costs. Forget about cash value concerns.

- **Unless it is specifically mandated under the conditions of the term policy's conversion section, you don't have to convert your entire term policy into one single permanent policy.** You could, for instance, convert your policy into two separate permanent policies: one to sell and the rest to keep as remaining life insurance coverage for your beneficiaries. You can also elect to convert only part of your coverage and have the insurance company issue you a term policy to cover the rest of the insurance value that you didn't convert. (Don't let that term coverage lapse, though. If you're just going to do that, you might as well convert it to a policy you can sell and get something back for it … unless, of course, you want to keep a little insurance capacity in your back pocket just in case you need it sometime down the road.)

Someone 65 or Older Without a Policy

There are many reasons why someone over 65 might want to buy large amount of life insurance, including estate planning, business succession concerns and charitable reasons. But you're probably reading this book because you're interested in buying life insurance to use as a personal investment. Some insurance companies and their representatives may try to convince you that there is something intrinsically wrong with this. There isn't. For many years, life insurance companies have been presenting a column on their policy illustrations called "Internal Rate of Return on Death Benefit". This column shows the insured that if they had died in a given year, what the rate of return on the death benefit paid to their beneficiary would be, relative to the premiums paid during the life of the insurance contract. In essence, this is showing an individual, a business, or a trustee how to utilize the death benefit as an investment for planning purposes. It makes perfect sense. If an insured is buying a policy, as an investment, to pay future estate taxes, wouldn't he or she want to know what the rate of return on the ultimate death benefit would be, relative to the premiums paid?

Still, the fact that some insurance companies don't much like life settlements means that you do need to be careful in how you go about the investment process. But if you do everything above board, legally and thoughtfully, there is no reason why you can't buy life insurance for use as an investment vehicle, even if you're over the age of 65.

A word of warning here: You are liable to find yourself regularly faced with the temptations of non-recourse premium financed and trustfront deals. There will be announcements for seminars on these things. There will be friends or family members who successfully entered into one of these arrangements and made off with a decent amount of money. There will be ads for brokers pushing these transactions and plenty of media stories about them. If you take nothing else from this book, we hope that you will see that neither non-recourse financing nor trustfront transactions are the best way to leverage your life insurance policy's investment potential. So step one of the Invest in Your Life process is simply this: Don't participate in a non-recourse or trustfront deal. Do this thing the right way and you'll earn a lot more money with less risk.

But first things first ... you need a life insurance policy. The obvious goal here is to get a policy with the highest possible face value for the lowest premium cost. There's nothing wrong with going to a life insurance broker to help you get a policy. If you do this, though, they will get a commission, and that commission will be added to your policy premium cost. So in effect, going to an insurance broker will cost you money. However, brokers do often have access to good deals based on your characteristics and risk classification. They are supposed to do your comparison shopping for you and present you with the best offers they find. And using a broker does save you a lot of legwork.

On the other hand, you could use the Internet to search for life insurance offers. Usually, an Internet search begins at quote sites like insure.com, ameritas.com or usaa.com. Just follow each site's instructions on how to obtain life insurance quotes. You could also contact individual insurance companies yourself and get quotes from them directly. In either case, you will likely find that premium costs are somewhat lower, since they won't have a heavy broker's commission loaded onto them. Even if you do use a broker, visiting these sites for quotes can't hurt just to see how the quotes you come across compare to those presented by your broker.

No matter how you go about getting your life insurance policy, there are some tips you should keep in mind when policy shopping:

- For investment, **the most desirable policy type is universal life.** So if you have strong intentions of selling your policy, do yourself a favor and stick to universal life. It is the easiest type of policy to sell, and it's worth the most on the market.

- **The policy's cash value options are of little importance.** Since you're planning on selling the policy anyway, there is little use in accruing any cash value. You probably won't be holding the policy long enough for the cash value to build up enough to be useful anyway.

- Obviously, the more face value you get on your policy, the more it'll be worth when you sell it. But you may not want to max out all your insurance capacity on one policy, especially if you plan on selling it. Instead, you might want to **consider splitting your insurance capacity into two separate policies: one for your beneficiaries and one for sale on the market.** Or you might elect to take out a policy that does not use all of your insurance capacity, allowing you to take out more insurance at a later date should the need for it arise.

- When comparing quotes, you should also **factor in the insurance company's rating.** An insurance company's Standard & Poor rating can be found for free at insure.com along with independent reports on that insurance company. Duff & Phelps also provide free access to insurer ratings at dcrco.com. Finally, free access to industry stalwart AM Best's ratings can be found at ambest.com.
  In general, these ratings are presented as something like letter grades. When choosing a policy to buy, try to **go with insurers who are rated an A or better** (with AAA usually marked as the highest grade). **When faced with two quotes that are close in price, always go with the offer from the higher rated company.** The rating of a policy's issuing insurance company is a factor in the life settlement price for that policy.

Someone Under 65 with an Active Permanent Policy

For a member of this group to be able to sell their policy, it usually means that he or she has a reduced life expectancy. Most often, this is because a life-threatening condition has been diagnosed. A longtime smoker might also occasionally fall into this group. As a rule of thumb, not even the most aggressive investors will look at anyone with a life expectancy that exceeds 200 months or about 17 years. Investors simply don't want to wait longer than that for a return on their investment. Also, the younger the insured, the less reliable any LE analysis is prone to be, so the less likely it is that an investor will gamble on the policy.

However, if a person under 65 has a life expectancy that is less than 200 months, it is possible that investors might be interested. Obviously, the lower the life expectancy, the better the chance that a younger policyholder will find a provider or investor to buy his or her policy. But if that life expectancy is two years or less, then the transaction falls under viatical law rather than life settlement guidelines.

In the end, unless a person under 65 has diagnosed health problems or a long history of smoking, there is little reason to try to settle a policy. Some life settlement brokers might ask: "Why not give it a shot? What have you got to lose?" Well, the only thing you've got to lose is time and effort. And since you've probably got a less than 1% chance of settling, you might as well spend that time polishing your shoes or shopping for bath towels … it'll be a lot more constructive. Instead, just wait a while. The market will be there waiting for you when you're ready for it, and it'll be even bigger and stronger than it is now.

Someone Under 65 with an Active Term Policy

This one is tricky, indeed. Providers and investors tend to turn their noses up at term policies under the best of circumstances, and if you're younger than 65, it's a long straw away from the best of circumstances. Unless you're looking at a viatical situation, chances are worse than poor that an investor will be interested in the term policy of a younger person. In fact, if you're in standard or better health, the only real advice here is to stay insured, protect the interests of your beneficiaries, and keep an eye on ways you can leverage your current coverage into future investment opportunity.

One problem is that term insurance will get more expensive each time you renew the term until the cost gets downright prohibitive. On the other hand, permanent insurance is more expensive than term insurance unless you are at a more advanced age. A good approach for someone of a younger age is to see if you can get the cheaper term insurance, but with a longer term coverage period—say, ten years or more. Then, make sure that the term coverage has a "Right to Convert" clause that includes a guarantee that your health risk classification will be preserved if you convert. This way, you can pay cheaper term rates until you want to sell the policy, and conversion won't result in a downgrade to your risk classification. The danger here is if you are still holding the policy when that long term runs out. At that point, you'll be older and possibly not in as good a shape healthwise, and you might find yourself very expensive to insure or uninsurable.

In contrast to a healthy under 65 policyholder, a person under 65 with a life expectancy of less than two years will often find interest in his or her policy from viatical companies. Even a term policy has a good chance of receiving interest under these circumstances. Just remember that these transactions fall under viatical law rather than statutes for life settlements.

If you do want to explore the possibility of selling your policy, the first step is to find out whether your term policy is convertible. Most—but not all—term policies are. In your policy's documentation, look for a section called "Right to Convert" or something similar. The terms for conversion will be outlined there. If you don't find that section or you need further clarification, you can always contact your insurance company.

When and if you decide to go through the pricing process, be sure to ask whether there's any advantage to converting. If you're looking at a viatical, you may find that you don't need to convert to sell the policy and that there's nothing to be gained by going through the conversion process. Still, it's a good idea to ask. You just may find that your policy will fetch a better price after it has been converted.

If you do decide to convert, there are some things you should know about the conversion process:

- **Most term policy conversions do not require a new medical exam.** We're sure you're saddened by this.

- **Many term policies are issued with a classification guarantee that enables you to convert to a permanent policy at the same health risk classification as your term policy.** If your health has taken a downward turn since you first got that term policy, you can still maintain your more favorable health classification when you convert without being underwritten at a lower, more expensive risk class.

- **On the other hand, if your health has improved since you first got your term insurance, you might want to go through medical underwriting again.** You could get bumped up to a more favorable risk class and save lots of money. Now that's worth a trip to the ole' doctor, isn't it?

- **You can only convert to a permanent policy with the same insurance company.** There's no switching teams in the middle of the game.

- **You may be limited as to which permanent plans you can convert to.** Because you are doing this for investment reasons, it is highly recommended that you convert to the type of policy that most investors are looking for—namely, universal life. If that isn't an option, whole life will do.

- **Because you plan on selling the policy, cash value isn't a concern.** If offered a choice between plans, choose one that maximizes face value while minimizing premium costs. Forget about cash value concerns.

- **Unless it is specifically mandated under the conditions of the term policy's conversion section, you don't have to convert your entire term policy into one single permanent policy.** You could, for instance, convert your policy into two separate permanent policies: one to sell and the rest to keep as remaining life insurance coverage for your beneficiaries. You can also elect to convert only part of your coverage and have the insurance company issue you a term policy to cover the rest of the insurance value that you didn't convert. (Don't let that term coverage lapse, though. If you're just going to do that, you might as well convert it to a policy you can sell and get something back for it … unless, of course, you want to keep a little insurance capacity in your back pocket just in case you need it sometime down the road.)

Someone Under 65 without a Policy

You are the proverbial clean slate. If you're under 65, you probably wouldn't be able to sell a policy unless you've already been diagnosed with a life-threatening condition. But if you've already been diagnosed with a life-threatening condition, you probably won't be able to get life insurance. All we can really do for you here is give you some of the most general advice about buying life insurance:

- For a younger person such as yourself, term insurance is generally cheaper than permanent insurance—sometimes drastically so. To cover traditional life insurance needs, it's often a good idea to buy a cheaper term policy. It's also a good idea to try to get a long insurable term, so that you can pay level premiums over a longer period of time without a price increase. However, make absolutely certain that the term policy is convertible. This way, you can convert the policy when you no longer need it and can sell it to the market. You also might want to make sure that you can convert it specifically to a universal life permanent policy, since that is the type desired most by investors.

- If you buy a permanent policy, keep in mind that cash value really is only best employed as a means for keeping your future premium costs down. It's a terrible investment vehicle, so don't use it as such no matter how much an insurance broker tries to convince you otherwise.

- Stay away from variable life. There are other ways to invest that provide better returns without risking your life insurance coverage. And investors don't much like variable life, either.

How to Invest in Your Life

Before we go through the step-by-step Invest in Your Life procedure, there are a few general points we need to review. First, remember that life settlement providers and investors are highly unlikely to work with policies that are valued at less than $200,000 at the moment. It's possible that as competition for policies continues to heat up, value requirements will loosen. But for now, holders of less valuable policies are really only likely to find any market interest if they have been diagnosed with a life-threatening condition that has reduced their life expectancy to two years or less. This, however, would make the transaction a viatical rather than a life settlement, so you would need to plan somewhat differently.

If you haven't been diagnosed with any condition that could significantly reduce your life expectancy and you have a policy worth less than $200,000, you might want to see if your insurance capacity could support an expansion of coverage to a value of at least $500,000 (preferably $1 million or more). You'll often earn a heck of a lot more back from the eventual policy sale than you'll pay over the next two years in additional premium costs. If you can medically and financially qualify for this amount of coverage, your beneficiary would then enjoy a significant payment should you decide to hold the policy until death.

During all of this, keep in mind that a life settlement is not an overnight process. Even if you decide to let brokers do a lot of the work for you (each taking a small piece of the investment along the way), you will still have to wait for the process to play itself out. A life settlement transaction can take as little as six weeks or fewer, but typically takes 8-12 weeks to come to completion, especially if the price comparisons take a long time. Additionally, there is due diligence that must be performed on your end to make sure that you are getting everything you can out of the settlement and that the entire transaction is being conducted legally, properly and in your best interest.

So the following is our Invest in Your Life process, complete with our official stamp of approval. What that all means is that these are our personal recommendations … neither more nor less. Follow these instructions and you will be going about the life settlement process in the best possible way to maximize your investment potential while minimizing your exposure to risk:

- The first step is to make sure your policy is seasoned. Sometimes, it can be tempting to try to sell a policy that is not yet fully seasoned, especially if you need money quickly. Resist this temptation. Many providers and investors will only buy seasoned policies, which is why wet policies are often worth so much less; the reduced market competition for that policy means it has a considerably lower market value. Plus, selling a wet policy puts the transaction in real danger of falling through if the insurance company rescinds the policy. This also applies if you recently added coverage value to your policy. If you just upgraded from $200,000 of coverage to $1 million, you should still wait two years after the upgrade before you consider selling your policy. Remember, your first option should always be to **consider keeping the policy and holding it until your death**. Once you sell the policy, you won't be able to buy it back, you will be utilizing your insurance capacity, and someone else will be making a pretty penny on the transaction.

If you have a permanent life insurance policy and need money immediately, there are better—and less costly—ways to leverage your policy than by pulling the trigger on a sale too early:

- Withdraw or borrow from cash value—If only a relatively small amount is needed immediately, you can withdraw or borrow that money from the policy's cash value account (assuming you have value built up in it). Usually, this will cost you some money in the form of withdrawal fees or loan interest, but the cost will often be less than borrowing money from a lending institution. To reduce tax and interest costs, the best process is to withdraw money from the cash value until its cost basis is reduced to $0. That is, don't withdraw more than you've paid in through premium payments. If you do, that which is withdrawn over the cost basis is taxable as income. A better choice would be to withdraw until the cost basis is $0, then borrow from the policy for the rest. Contact your insurance company for details on this.

- Borrow from a bank using your policy as collateral—Your permanent life insurance policy is high-level collateral since a lender can be assured of repayment when its death benefit pays out. As a result, you can often use it as collateral to get yourself a loan with a very reasonable interest rate.

However it is you decide to borrow money, keep this in mind—do **not** do anything that could risk your policy lapsing. This includes borrowing so much from cash value that you can't afford paying policy premiums anymore. If you do let your policy lapse, you lose your entire investment. To regain your coverage, you'll have to purchase insurance again, and this time it'll be more expensive. And that's only if you can still get coverage at all. So—one last time for emphasis—**don't let that policy lapse!**

- If you have a permanent policy with cash value built up in it, **you need to know your policy's surrender value**. This will give you a sort of baseline figure as to how much your policy is worth right now without even taking the secondary market into consideration. Also, **find out what your cash value's current rate of investment return is**. This will tell you how much your policy will be worth in the future. When and if you do sell your policy, you obviously want to get a whole lot more for it than the surrender value it's currently worth and its projected value going forward.

- **You may want to use some external third-party resources to price your policy.** Using these can give you a good idea of the sort of prices providers should be offering you. Everything from simple online policy pricing tools to contact information for individuals willing to perform deep, complex valuation analyses can be found on the Internet. We can't list these resources because we don't want to give the impression that we're endorsing one of these over another. However, keep in mind that no matter how thorough the analysis from one of these resources seems, it is still only useful as a preliminary step in your policy pricing process. You can use the numbers you get from these resources as a jumping off point from which you can begin negotiations with brokers and providers, but those brokers and providers are ultimately the only pricing authorities that matter. If a third-party resource says your policy is worth X dollars, but no one offers you anywhere near X dollars for it, then your policy isn't worth X dollars no matter what that resource says. Your policy is only worth what the market will pay.

- The next step is to **contact your state's insurance commissioner's**

office. Every state (and the District of Columbia) has one. All of these commissions have websites, and some of these are excellent resources for information on life settlements and viaticals in your state. While these commissions are a wealth of general useful information which you absolutely should avail yourself of before entering into a settlement, you will want to contact your state's commission for two specific reasons:

- First, because life settlement and viatical legislation is all state-based, **you will need to find the laws particular to your state** before you proceed. We would love to print them all here, but life settlement laws are different from state to state. At last count, we've got a good, solid fifty states in this sizable country of ours. That's an awful lot of ink—maybe worth a book or two by itself. And those laws are changing so rapidly that what we printed here would probably have been woefully obsolete by the time you read it. Instead, we're going to have to point you to the state commission, which obviously has all the latest information on your state's life settlement laws.

- **The commissioner's office also can tell you whether a life settlement broker or provider has to be licensed or certified in that state.** If so, the commissioner will usually have a list of the state's licensed life settlement brokers and providers, as well as their contact information. This list may also include the number of complaints that have been filed against a particular broker or provider, so it can be a spectacularly handy reference tool both to find potential contacts and to determine the quality of those contacts.

At the end of this book, you'll find Appendix A, which contains the contact information and website address for every state insurance commission (and, of course, the District of Columbia).

- Your next task is to make a decision. **You have to choose whether or not you want to use a life settlement broker to help you with the arrangements or whether you want to go it alone and approach providers yourself.** The advantage to using a broker is convenience; the broker will help set up the paperwork and will do most of your legwork for you as it is the broker's primary task to pursue and compare offers between the different providers. The disadvantage, of course, is cost. A broker doesn't do these things for free and will take a piece of your investment return in some form or other. How much the broker takes varies from broker to broker, but the broker's slice can range from fairly modest to titanic. For your bottom line, it is obviously better to avoid brokers altogether. However, you may find that the time a broker saves you is worth all of the money it costs. The choice, ultimately, is yours.

If you decide you do want to use a life settlement broker, here are some tips on how to find a good apple in the barrel:

- **Use your state's insurance commission to locate a broker.** Make sure you find out if the commission will reveal if the broker you're looking at has ever received any complaints.

- **The broker should be licensed to conduct life settlements in your state**, assuming that your state provides licenses for life settlements. Most do.

- **The broker must adhere to the code of ethics and conduct mandated by LISA (the Life Insurance Settlement Association).** This code includes full disclosure of all commissions, fees and compensation being deducted from the policy's *gross offer*. The gross offer is the total amount a provider or investor is willing to pay for the policy. The code also mandates that the broker diligently price the secondary market to find the highest gross offer possible for the policy. The life settlement broker has a fiduciary responsibility to work in your best interest.

- **You should never be assessed a fee just for a consultation visit.** If a broker demands one, it's a deal-breaker. Don't work with them. Ever.

- **Discover how long the broker has been in business.** Remember, though, life settlements are a relatively new industry. Any broker that has been around four years or more is an industry veteran. This doesn't necessarily mean that they are a top-notch broker, but it is one factor to consider.

- **Get a list of referrals from the broker.** This one is pretty self-explanatory.

- **Find out how many providers a broker deals with.** If it seems that a broker is pushing one particular provider too hard, he or she might have an arrangement with that provider and might not be working in your best interest. Find another broker. Nowadays, life settlement brokers are getting as easy to find as pigeons in a park.

- **Ask what type of commission or fee the broker demands for their services.** It should never, ever, ever exceed 6% of the policy's face value (and that's steep!). If a broker asks for a third of your total settlement, avoid that broker like a leper with the flu.

- **Does the broker provide good, detailed information about itself? Does it focus its business on life settlements? Does the broker have an anti-fraud policy?** These answers should always be Yes, Yes and Yes.

- If you live in a state where life settlement transactions are not regulated, **you may want to consider using a broker from a state known for having strict, tight life settlement laws and regulations.** Some of these states would be New York, Florida, California and Washington.

If you're the do-it-yourself type and decide to forego the aid of a broker in favor of a higher return on your investment, you're going to have to shop your policy around to various providers yourself. This isn't necessarily as daunting as it may sound, but it does involve more work from your end. Here a little list of helpful hints on how to go about this most efficiently:

- **See if you can use your state's insurance commission to locate providers.** Also, find out if the commission has any records on the provider and see if it has ever received any complaints.

- If you can't get a list of providers from your state commissioner's office, **you may be able to find providers through the Internet or other advertising channels.** Obviously, you need to be extra careful of any provider you find through this means, so really dig deep to make sure that this is a provider you can trust.

- Once you have found some providers you'd like to contact, **check your state's attorney general's office to see if there has ever been any legal action against the provider.**

- **Only work with a provider that is institutionally funded.** The more reputable the funding, the more secure you can feel when working with that provider.

- **Check a provider's experience and volume.** A good provider should have several years' experience in the life settlement space and should have purchased a solid $500 million in policy face value before you consider them.

- **Stick to providers that have a good *Scope rating*.** A Scope rating is a score assigned by the Scope Group, a German investment rating agency. The Scope Group has increasingly rated North American life settlement providers for German investors, but their ratings are just as valuable for American investors.

- **Remember, while a broker works for you, a provider's representative works only for that provider.** It is not their responsibility to provide you with a best offer. It is up to you to leverage your negotiating power. And you have a lot of it. The life settlement market is hungry for policies. Use that knowledge to get yourself the best deal you can.

- Perhaps most importantly of all, **don't just sign on with the first provider that looks good.** Just because they meet all of these criteria doesn't mean that they'll give you a good price for your policy. Whittle your list of possible providers down to only those that look the most solid, but then make sure you get a price from all of those solid-looking providers. Your goal is to field as many bids as you can from as many solid, reputable providers as possible, then see if you can negotiate upward from there. You may even be able to use one provider's bid against another to get them to raise their offer.

Whether you use a broker or go about it the do-it-yourself way, remember that while a referral from a friend or family member is helpful, it is by no means the last word. You must perform your due diligence in checking up on any broker or provider. There's too much money involved here to rely entirely on your brother-in-law's friend's recommendation.

- Once you have chosen the offer you want to go with, there are some things you must consider before you sell:

- **The sale is irreversible after ten or fifteen days, depending on the arrangement,** so be careful when you finally do pull that trigger.

- Consider this: **Do you really want to give away the coverage that secures your beneficiaries?** Again, once you decide, it's a one-way deal—there's no going back. You really must talk it over with your beneficiaries first to make sure that they aren't counting on that death benefit.

- Once you sell your policy, you have sold at least a portion—if not all—of your insurance capacity. **If you are concerned about this, you might want to split your policy, sell a portion away and keep the other portion in force. Or you may elect to sell a policy that does not exhaust all of your insurance capacity,** leaving the rest uninsured for the moment but available if you decide to acquire insurance to cover that remaining capacity at a later date.

- When you consider the various offers on the table, **make sure you factor in all the costs and fees—don't just look at the gross offer.**

- **Don't—and we really mean this—give away any significant portion of the final settlement to a broker.** No broker is worth a third of the settlement.

- Before selling to an investor, you might want to **consider selling your policy to an heir or relative.** You can get some ready cash, and they can hang onto the death benefit. It may be the best thing for everybody.

- If you have a life expectancy of less than two years, **see if your policy offers accelerated death benefits.** If it does, see how that number compares to the offers you are getting for a viatical settlement. You may be surprised to find that the insurance company will pay you more for your policy than those investors.

- If you have a life expectancy of less than two years, you can also **look at combining your policy's accelerated death benefit (if it has one) with a viatical settlement.** Sometimes this will provide a higher rate of return than just doing either alone.

- If your policy doesn't get any offers right away, **don't panic.** Just hang in there. Look at this as a "wait and see" investment. As you age and your life expectancy shortens, the policy will become more desirable and offers will come in. Don't surrender or lapse that policy—that's a money-losing proposition every time.

- Finally, if you decide to hold the policy until your death, you should periodically check on its status. You can do this by calling your agent, broker, or the company from which the insurance was purchased. When checking its status, make sure that the policy is currently in force and get a projection of the future premiums necessary to keep the policy in force for life. Again, you do not want the policy to lapse!

10

Q & A: The Invest in Your Life Question and Answer Session

Okay, so we've put it all out there and given you our best advice. Know what? If you've read this book all the way through, you probably know more about this stuff than a lot of people in the insurance industry. And that's no exaggeration.

But you may still have some doubts, some questions, may feel that there are some concerns that need addressing. Since this is a book, not a seminar, we can't really hear you ask those questions. The best we can do is guess what those questions might be and answer them without you having to ask. It's clear evidence of our psychic powers. It also demonstrates the kind of questions we most often hear when clients ask us about life settlements ...

Q: Once and for all, are life settlements legal?
Short answer: Yes.

Long answer: We're not going to bore you to tears with all of the legal nitty gritty—which, believe us, is painfully substantial in volume—but all legal arguments basically boil down to a couple of landmark pieces of legal sorcery.

The first originated all the way back in 18th century England.

Back then, it was a common practice for an individual to essentially buy a term life insurance policy on a stranger without the "insured" person ever even knowing that a policy had been taken out on his or her life. For all intents and purposes, life insurance became nothing more than a betting wager. If the "insured" person died during the coverage period, the individual who bought the policy—the "investor," of sorts—won the wager and pocketed the benefit payout. What is peculiar is just how unlucky many of these "insured" people were. They just seemed to suffer tragic accident after tragic accident, dying off in droves while the "investors" made lots of money. It grew to such epidemic proportions that becoming insured was pretty much the same as having a price on your head.

111

Eventually, Parliament had to step in and put a stop to all the malfeasance. Their response was the passage of the widely ballyhooed Life Assurance Act of 1774, often called the 1774 Gambling Act.

What the Gambling Act basically said in a nutshell was that a) a person who was not buying a policy for himself or herself could only buy a policy on someone else if they showed a level of insurable interest in the continued life of the insured—that is, the purchaser had to show that they had something to gain by the insured continuing to live (i.e. a spouse, a child, a business partner, etc.); b) an insured person always had to be aware of the fact that a policy had been taken out on his or her life.

This law would eventually become the foundation upon which all insurable interest laws would be built. Even today, the insurable interest laws in most states are largely based on this single piece of 240 year-old British legislation.

Fast forward nearly a hundred fifty years or so …

At the turn of the 20th century, the question of life insurance policy ownership was still a big problem. It became so hotly debated in the United States that it made it all the way to the Supreme Court. There, in the seminal Grigsby vs. Russell decision, the Supreme Court determined that a life insurance policy was the property of the policyholder and, as such, adhered strictly to property law. That meant that a legal owner of a life insurance policy could transfer ownership of that policy in any way they saw fit—including sale to an investor—just like any other piece of property.

If it seems to you like the Gambling Act's insurable interest laws and the Grigsby vs. Russell Supreme Court decision simply cannot coexist in the same legal universe, you're not alone. Each has its passionate backers—namely, insurance companies for the former and investors for the latter—who may well be battling tooth and nail in some courtroom somewhere over this issue this very moment.

But as is so often the case in these sorts of things, the great majority of the legal world has found a compromise. To prevent abuse of insurable interest laws, only the prospective insured or someone with an insurable interest in the prospective insured can initially buy the policy from the insurance company. Fair enough. However, to accommodate the Grigsby vs. Russell decision, it is perfectly acceptable from a legal standpoint to transfer ownership of that policy, including through the sale of the policy. But to prevent people from simply buying a policy, then "flipping" it right over to an investor, ownership of a policy does not really become "official" until it has survived the contestability period—that is, a policyholder's ownership of a policy does not become incontestable until after two years.

And there it is ... the great compromise that makes life settlements possible. Over time, the legal debate has begun to shift and settle on other things, such as seeding techniques and application fraud. The Great Life Insurance Compromise is well on its way to being regarded as established legal fact, if it isn't there already. And with a soon-to-be $160 billion industry built on the back of this compromise, don't even imagine for one second that the legal world's position is going to change now.

Um ... so, yeah ... life settlements are legal.

Now just imagine if we'd left in the *really* long answer we originally had in here ...

Q: If life settlements have been legal since Grigsby v. Russell, how come they're so new? Wouldn't people have been selling their policies pretty much through most of the 20th century?
A: Now that's a great question and we're glad you asked it.

The truth is viaticals and life settlements are relatively new to us here in the U.S. but have been around longer elsewhere. A legitimate secondary market for life insurance has existed in England almost since the passage of the 1774 Life Assurance Act. In Germany, life insurance policies have been bought by investors since the late eighties. Throughout the nineties, many individual German investors actually financed their retirements by purchasing life insurance policies from Irish and English policyholders. So why did it take so long to catch on here in the United States? Honestly, we can't say. But life settlements have caught on so quickly and the industry has already grown so large that you almost get the impression that the market has every intention of making up for lost time.

Q: I don't have a policy right now, but I'm afraid to get one because I'm not certain that this market will exist in two years when I can sell it. So ... lemme ask you this, Mr. Psychic ... will there still be a secondary market for life insurance in two years?
A: Lots of things can happen in two years. A meteor could hit the Earth. The polar ice caps could suddenly melt away and turn Idaho into beachfront. The world could be invaded by giant chipmunks. But barring a disaster of these proportions, there will surely be a secondary market for life insurance. How do we know? Because Berkshire Hathaway, JP Morgan Chase, Royal Bank of Scotland, and Deutsche Bank—among many other big names—are investing billions of dollars in this market. These aren't companies that squeeze their eyes shut, roll the dice and hope for the best. If big-name, fiscally conservative investment giants feel secure enough in the market's future to splash out

billions of dollars on it—literally, billions—then the fact that the market will still be around two years from now is pretty much a certainty.

Sanford C. Bernstein & Company estimated that $13 billion worth of policies were purchased in 2005. They estimate that $160 billion worth of policies will be purchased in 2030. That's more than a twelve-fold increase in market size over the next 25 years. That hardly indicates a market that has any intention of going away.

Besides, we're psychic. We know these things.

Q: I don't like the notion of selling away all of my insurance capacity and leaving my beneficiaries with nothing. Is there any way I could keep a portion of the benefit for my beneficiaries and sell only part of my policy?
A: Absolutely. The answer is called policy splitting. You can essentially have your policy split into two parts, one of which you sell to a provider and the other of which you hold onto as traditional life insurance protection for your beneficiaries. Most brokers or providers will be willing to discuss this option with you.

Q: How do I know that my policy isn't being sold to Tony Soprano Inc. and that I'm not going to get whacked as soon as the investor buys my policy? All those people back in 18th century England had tragic "accidents," too. How do I know that someone won't shoot me stone dead just to make their investment pay off?
A: Unlike 18th century England, the identity of any person involved in a life settlement transaction is held in strict confidence. While the health information about settlors is made available to prospective investors, all other personal identifiers such as name, address or any other piece of personal information is kept secret. This level of confidentiality is at the same level as a bank keeping your financial information secret or a credit card company guarding your credit card number. Any broker or provider who revealed any of this information would find themselves in very serious violation of confidentiality law. So, to answer the question you would've asked had you been able to ask a question at all, Tony Soprano would never have any idea whose policy he had invested in, so he would have no idea who to whack to make his investment pay out faster.

Q: Is it possible that my policy won't sell on the secondary market?
A: Well, yes. The secondary market is like any other marketplace—it adheres to laws of supply and demand, to external market pressures, and to laws of

competition and pricing. If your policy isn't attractive enough to buyers, it won't get bought. But there are two things to remember here ...

First, this market has grown explosively. At this point, there just aren't enough policies out there to meet the insatiable demand of investors. This means that the standards for what constitutes an acceptable policy for the market are liable to get more lenient, not tighter, over time.

Second, as you get older, your life expectancy gets shorter. As your life expectancy gets shorter, your policy gets more attractive to the market. The cure for a policy that isn't selling is usually just to sit and wait. Try again a year later and see. Quite often, that one year of waiting is all it takes. And if not, just wait again. Eventually, your policy will have takers, assuming it has a face value of at least $200,000 (though more is better).

11

Give and Take: The Tax Implications of Your Life Settlement

It probably won't come as a big surprise to you that the government is fully intent on taking a juicy bite out of your life settlement. That much is certain. But exactly how big that bite is going to be ... well, that's another story.

The problem is that tax experts and assessors still disagree on how life settlements should be taxed. Also, because life settlements are regulated on a state-by-state basis, there are variations in tax practices between states, too. The end result is the somewhat hard-to-swallow notion that a life settlement may be taxed differently based on what state you live in and who is doing the assessing.

Fortunately, a standard practice does appear to be rising from all the confusion ...

First of all, the sale of a life insurance policy has been pretty conclusively established as a taxable event. Some in the life settlement industry tried to claim that a life insurance policy sale should be tax-free, just like most death benefit payouts. That would be nice, but that's not the direction it went. If you sell it, they will tax it. Count on it.

You need two pieces of information to take the next step in assessing your tax liability: how much you have paid in premiums to keep the policy in force (your *cost of insurance*) and the policy's surrender value. Now compare the two figures.

Your policy's surrender value will usually be higher than your cost of insurance when your policy has cash value built up in it. If this is the case for you, there is good news and not so good news. The good news is that your life settlement will usually be tax-free up until the cost of insurance. After that comes the sort of bad news: your settlement will usually be taxed as normal income up until the surrender value of the policy. The rest of the sale is then normally taxed as capital gains.

Let's take a $2 million policy that sells for $1.2 million. The policyholder had paid $700,000 or so in premiums on the policy. It has a little over $100,000 in cash value built up in it, so the surrender value of the policy is around $800,000. In this instance, the most common tax methodology would dictate that the first $700,000 of the settlement would be tax-free, the next $100,000 or so taxed as normal income, and the remaining $400,000 taxed as capital gains.

If, however, the policy's surrender value is less than the cost of insurance, the settlement is often only tax-free up until the surrender value, not the cost of insurance. Any money that comes in from the policy sale that is above the surrender value is then taxed as capital gains.

While this may be the most common tax method applied to life settlements, it is unfortunately still not a locked-down standard. It is therefore exceptionally important to check with a tax advisor in your state to make sure that the tax implications follow along these lines. If not, you'll need your tax advisor to help you comply with your state's standards—whatever those may be.

Glossary

accelerated death benefits—payments paid out by a life insurance company to an insured person who has a life expectancy of less than two years. The accelerated death benefits are in proportion to the death benefit that person's beneficiaries would receive, i.e. a person with a life insurance policy worth $2 million may be able to get an accelerated death benefit payout totaling 70% of their policy's death benefit payout or $1.4 million. Accelerated death benefits are often abbreviated as *ADBs*.

accumulation fund—the cash value reserve of a universal life policy

actuarial table—see *mortality table*

actuary—a statistical analyst for an insurance company who calculates risk, establishes rules for classification, and sets policy pricing

ADBs—see *accelerated death benefits*

APS—see *Attending Physician Statement*

Attending Physician Statement—documents filled out by a doctor attesting to the health of a patient. In life insurance, these are usually completed by the doctor after a medical exam during the application process. Often abbreviated as *APS*.

beneficiary—in life insurance, a recipient of a policy's death benefit

benefit—the payout an insurance company has to make when a legitimate claim is submitted

capacity—see *insurance capacity*

cash value—a cash reserve associated with a permanent life insurance policy. A portion of a policy's premium payments goes into that policy's cash value. This stored money is applied later in the life of the policy to keep policy premium costs down when they would normally increase due to the advancing age of the insured. Cash value accounts usually gain interest value just like a savings account. How that value is accrued and how the cash value is applied to keep premium costs down depend on the type of insurance policy.

classification—see *risk classification*

collateral loan—In contrast to a nonrecourse loan, a collateral loan necessitates the borrower to put up some property as collateral in case he or she defaults on the loan. Often, the terms for collateral loans are more favorable than those for nonrecourse loans.

contestability—the principle that a life insurance company can rescind a policy within the first two years it is in force if it suspects that a material misrepresentation occurred on the insured's application. After two years, the insurance company can only rescind a policy if it proves that a fraud occurred, which demands a heavier burden of legal proof.

contestability clause—the portion of a life insurance policy's legal contract that outlines the contestability principle

conversion—see *policy conversion*

death benefit—the payout a life insurance company has to make when a legitimate claim is submitted

face value—the value of a policy's death benefit. Often just referred to as the *value* of the policy.

file audit—an insurance company procedure where a policyholder's insurance application and records are carefully scrutinized to look for inconsistencies. If problems are found, the policy may be rescinded and legal action may even be taken. If an insurance company believes a policy is being used for a SOLI/IOLI deal, it may perform a file audit on the policy.

forced savings—when a portion of a payment for a service is put into a cash reserve without the customer's say-so. In the case of life insurance, a permanent policy's cash value is an example of forced savings.

fraud—when someone fabricates or omits information on their insurance application. From a legal standpoint, fraud is more difficult to prove (and a more serious offence) than material misrepresentation.

Gambling Act—see *Life Assurance Act*

grantor—the party who grants an asset to be held in trust by a trustee until the conditions of the trust document have been met.

Grigsby vs. Russell—a landmark U.S. Supreme Court decision which ruled that life insurance policies were property of the policyholder and, as such, standard property laws could be applied to them. As a result, the transfer of policy ownership was legally sanctioned under property law.

gross offer—the total amount an investor or a provider will pay for a policy. This figure does not factor in any commission charges, administration fees, etc.

HIPAA—the Health Insurance Portability and Accountability Act passed by Congress in 1996. Among many other things, HIPAA protects the privacy of health records, and so forms and procedures that open these records to insurance companies during the application process must comply with HIPAA standards.

IILI—see *Investor Initiated Life Insurance*

in force—the state of an insurance policy that is active. If the premiums for a policy are up-to-date, the policy is in force.

incontestability—the principle that a life insurance company must prove a fraud occurred in order to rescind a policy that has been in force for more than two years. Prior to two years, the insurance company must only prove that a material misrepresentation occurred, which carries a lighter burden of proof.

incontestability clause—see *contestability clause*

insurable interest—the legal principle that a policy's beneficiaries must have something to gain financially in the continued life of the insured or something to lose financially in the event of that person's death

insurance capacity—the maximum amount of life insurance coverage a person can have. This figure is based on a person's net worth and an insurance company's individual practices. Often, a person's insurance capacity is set at 80% of their total net worth. Also just called *capacity*.

Investor Initiated Life Insurance—a term used to describe life insurance policies sold to individuals already signed up for a life settlement. Sometimes abbreviated as *IILI*.

Investor Owned Life Insurance—a term applied when a life insurance policyholder is an investor in that policy, not the insured or someone with an insurable interest in the insured. The investor will wait for the insured to pass away in order to collect the death benefit. Different from a *SOLI* case only in that the policyholder must be an organized investor. Often abbreviated as *IOLI*.

IOLI—see *Investor Owned Life Insurance*

key person contracts—life insurance policies taken out on individuals who are indispensable to a company in order to insure that company against the damage and difficulty caused by the death of that individual

lapse rate—the planned rate at which an insurance company expects policyholders to allow their insurance coverage to lapse—or go inactive—by either canceling or not paying. In life insurance, a lapse rate that is too high means the company is getting too little income in premium payments. A lapse rate that is too low means the company is paying out too many death benefits.

LE—see *life expectancy analysis*

level premiums—premium payments that stay the same for the life of coverage. A person with a level premium permanent insurance policy will pay the same premium payments as long as the policy stays in force. Level premiums for term insurance last until the term expires.

LexNet exchange—a large electronic trading exchange hosted by Cantor Fitzgerald and designed exclusively for the life settlement industry

Life Assurance Act—a piece of legislation passed by the British Parliament in 1774 that established the principle of insurable interest. Still used as the basis for insurable interest laws in the United States today. Also called the *Gambling Act.*

life expectancy analysis—a statistical analysis performed on a potential settlor using APS reports and other medical records to estimate life expectancy. In life settlements, this is often performed by third-party companies that specialize in this sort of analysis. Often abbreviated as *LE.*

Life Insurance Settlement Association—An organization dedicated to raising awareness and establishing standardized best practices for the life settlement industry. Abbreviated as *LISA.*

life settlement—A life settlement is where a third-party investor buys a life insurance policy from a policyholder with a life expectancy of more than two years. Sometimes the investor will hold the policy to collect the death benefit when that person passes on. Other times, the investor will turn around and resell the policy to another investor.

life table—see *mortality table*

LISA—see *Life Insurance Settlement Association*

load—additional costs that are built into the premium payments for a policy. Some examples of load costs would be insurance commissions, administrative fees, etc.

material misrepresentation—when someone fabricates or omits information on their insurance application. From a legal standpoint, material misrepresentation is easier to prove (and a lesser offence) than fraud.

maturation—a term sometimes used when a death benefit pays out. Often used when the policyholder is an investor.

miracle cure effect—when advances in medical treatment enable those afflicted with a particular condition to enjoy longer life expectancies. For secondary market life insurance investors, this can cause a sharp drop in investment profitability, especially if the investor over-invested in policies belonging to people suffering from a single condition.

Model Act—see *Model Viatical Settlement Act*

Model Viatical Settlement Act—the first piece of legislation created by NAIC to govern and establish standards for viatical settlements. Its principles would later be applied to life settlements as well. Sometimes just called the *Model Act* in the insurance industry.

mortality charge—the portion of a life insurance premium that covers the insurance company's *net amount at risk*. This is the actual cost of insurance. The remaining portion of the premium is usually a contribution to the policy's cash value reserve.

mortality table—a tool used by actuaries to assess insurance risk. Given a particular set of characteristics (i.e. age, gender, smoker or non-smoker, etc.), the mortality table shows the statistical probability that someone who fits those characteristics will die during the next year. Also called a *life table* or an *actuarial table*.

NAIC—see *National Association of Insurance Commissioners*

National Association of Insurance Commissioners—an association of industry professionals that produces standards that govern the insurance industry. Often abbreviated as *NAIC*.

net amount at risk—the part of a death benefit that comes out of the insurance company's own pocket rather than the portion that comes from a policy's cash value

nonrecourse loan—a high-interest loan where the only collateral is the item for which the money is being borrowed, e.g. a piece of real estate or a life insurance policy. If the borrower defaults on the loan, the lender has no legal right—or recourse—to any other borrower property other than the collateral item.

nonrecourse premium financing—a life settlement seeding technique using nonrecourse loans to provide two years of "free" life insurance to the settlor. This almost always results in the settlor receiving less return for the policy sale.

ordinary life—see *whole life*

permanent insurance—insurance coverage without a time limit. As long as premium payments are made, a permanent policy stays in force.

phantom income—If a nonrecourse life settlement transaction falls through, it's possible to get taxed on the money that was borrowed to perform the deal, even though the deal was never completed.

policy conversion—changing a term life insurance policy into a permanent policy. Often just referred to as *conversion*.

policy splitting—taking part of a policy's value and selling it to a provider or investor while keeping the rest. For example, a policyholder may take a policy worth $5 million, sell $3 million to an investor and keep the remaining $2 million in force to cover estate taxes, burial costs, etc. Sometimes just called *splitting*.

policyholder—the owner of an insurance policy. This is the person who pays the policy's premiums. The policyholder is not always the insured, e.g. after a life settlement transaction, the investor is the policyholder, not the insured.

pooling strategies—an investment technique designed to reduce risk. In life settlements, investors will usually hold many policies so that if a few exceed life expectancies and provide low or no investment return, the rest will make up the difference and virtually guarantee a positive investment return on the pool.

preferred—at many insurance companies, the most desirable risk class for an insured person. It means the person poses less of a financial risk to the insurance company than most people, and so that person can pay less than insured people in other risk classes.

preferred plus—the best risk classification for an insured person in those companies that offer this risk class. A preferred plus insured person poses a far lower financial risk to the insurance company, and so coverage will be much less expensive than for a standard risk person.

premium—a regular payment paid to insurers to keep an insurance policy in force. The cost of an insurance policy. If you stop paying a policy's premiums, that policy lapses.

provider—in the life settlement industry, a company that sets up a viatical or life settlement by communicating with a potential viator or settlor, purchasing his or her policy, then either holding it or turning it around and selling it to investors for a profit

rescind—when an insurance company ends its coverage before a policy's term expires. Usually, this is because of a legal challenge resulting from a perceived misrepresentation or fraud on the application for insurance.

risk classification—the process of putting prospective insurance applicants into groups that represent different levels of risk to the insurance company. The usual risk classes are preferred, standard and substandard, though some insurance companies also have a high-end preferred plus class as well. Also just called *classification*.

Scope rating—a score assigned by the Scope Group, a German investment rating agency that rates North American life settlement providers

seasoned policy—a policy that has been in force for more than two years and so has aged past its contestability period

secondary market—in life insurance, the investors and providers willing to buy second-hand life insurance policies as investments

seeding—techniques employed by life settlement agents and providers to entice policyholders into life settlement transactions. Nonrecourse premium financing is a seeding technique. Seeding techniques have been the target of legal challenges and usually result in a lower return for the settlor.

settlor—the insured person in a life settlement

SOLI—see *Stranger Owned Life Insurance*

Speculator Initiated Life Insurance—a term used to describe life insurance policies sold to individuals already signed up for a life settlement. Sometimes abbreviated as *SPINLIFE*.

SPINLIFE—see *Speculator Initiated Life Insurance*

splitting—see *policy splitting*

standard—the average risk classification for an insured person. A standard insured poses an average financial risk to the insurance company. Most insured people fall into this classification.

straight life—see *whole life*

Stranger Owned Life Insurance—a term applied when a life insurance policyholder is neither the insured nor someone with an insurable interest in the insured. Used in reference to insurance coverage held by someone who is waiting for the insured to pass away in order to collect the death benefit. Often abbreviated as *SOLI*.

substandard—a below average risk classification for an insured person. This person would pose a greater than average financial risk to the insurance company. Someone deemed a substandard risk may be denied coverage if applying or will pay more for insurance than a standard risk.

surrender—willful canceling of a life insurance policy. When a policy is canceled, the policyholder will receive any cash value that has built up, minus any surrender charges that are due.

surrender value—the total, final value of a policy that has been surrendered. The surrender value is calculated by taking a policy's cash value plus accrued interest and subtracting all surrender charges.

term—the length of time for which insurance coverage is provided

term insurance—insurance coverage with an expiration date. Terms can be of varying lengths, but will eventually run out and require the insured to actively renew coverage if continued coverage is desired.

trust—a legally binding arrangement under which an asset is assigned by a grantor to a trustee who holds it until the conditions established in a trust document are met. At that point, the trustee gives the asset to the trust's beneficiary. In the secondary life insurance market, the grantor is usually the policyholder; the asset is the life insurance policy; the beneficiary is the investor.

trust document—the legally binding instructions given to a trustee that define the conditions under which the asset placed in trust must be granted to the beneficiaries

trustee—the caretaker and administrator of a trust. When the conditions of the trust document are met, the trustee gives the asset held in trust over to the trust's beneficiaries.

trustfront deal—a life settlement technique using a trust, which makes it difficult for insurance companies to know when a policy changes ownership. Designed to get around insurable interest laws.

underwriting—the process of assessing the risk an insurance applicant poses to the insurer

universal life—a type of permanent life insurance policy. The cash value of a universal life policy is called the *accumulation fund*. It grows at a variable rate but is guaranteed to never drop below a fixed rate of return. It cannot lose value.

value—see *face value*

variable life—a type of permanent life insurance policy. The cash value is assigned to an aggressive investment portfolio that can lose value, putting the life insurance policy at risk if the investments perform badly.

viatical settlement—an arrangement where a third-party investor buys a life insurance policy from a policyholder with a life expectancy of two years or less in order to collect the death benefit when that person passes on. Also simply called a viatical.

viator—the insured person in a viatical settlement

wet ink deal—a risky life settlement transaction that is performed using a wet policy.

wet policy—a policy that is less than two years old so that it has not yet aged past its contestability period

whole life—a type of permanent life insurance policy. The cash value builds up through a fixed interest rate. It cannot lose value. Also sometimes called *ordinary life* or *straight life*.

APPENDIX A

State Insurance Commissioners' Contact Information

Alabama

Alabama Department of Insurance
201 Monroe Street, Suite 1700
Montgomery, AL 36104
334-269-3550
http://www.aldoi.gov

Alaska

Alaska Division of Insurance
Robert B. Atwood Building
550 West Seventh Avenue, Suite 1560
Anchorage, AK 99501-3067
907-269-7900
http://www.dced.state.ak.us/insurance

Arkansas
Arkansas Insurance Department
1200 West Third Street
Little Rock, AR 72201
800-282-9134
http://www.state.ar.us/insurance

Arizona

Arizona Department of Insurance
2910 North 44th Street, Second Floor
Phoenix, AZ 85018-7256

602-912-8444 (Phoenix)
520-628-6370 (Tucson)
800-325-2548 (rest of state)
http://www.id.state.az.us

California

California Department of Insurance
300 South Spring Street, South Tower
Los Angeles, CA 90013
800-927-4357
http://www.insurance.ca.gov

Colorado

Colorado Division of Insurance
1560 East Broadway, Suite 850
Denver, CO 80202
303-894-7499
303-894-7490 (consumer information)
http://www.dora.state.co.us/insurance/

Connecticut

Connecticut Insurance Department
P.O. Box 816
Hartford, CT 06142-0816
860-297-3800
800-203-3447 (Connecticut only)
http://www.ct.gov/cid/site/default.asp

Delaware

Delaware Insurance Department
841 Silver Lake Boulevard
Dover, DE 19904
302-739-4251
http://www.state.de.us/inscom

District of Columbia

District of Columbia Department of Insurance,
 Securities and Banking
810 First Street Northwest, Suite 701
Washington, DC 20002
202-727-8000
http://www.disr.washingtondc.gov
Florida

Florida Department of Financial Services
Office of Insurance Regulation
200 East Gaines Street
Tallahassee, FL 32399-0333
800-342-2762
http://www.fldfs.com
Georgia

Georgia Insurance and Safety Fire Commissioner
2 Martin Luther King, Jr. Drive
West Tower, Suite 704
Atlanta, GA 30334
800-656-2298
http://www.inscomm.state.ga.us/

Hawaii

Hawaii Division of Insurance
P.O. Box 3614
Honolulu, HI 96811
808-586-2790
http://www.state.hi.us/dcca/ins

Idaho

Idaho Department of Insurance
P.O. Box 83720
Boise, ID 83720-0043
208-334-4250
http://www.doi.state.id.us

Illinois

Illinois Department of Insurance
James R. Thompson Center
100 West Randolph Street, Suite 5-570
Chicago, IL 60601-3251
312-814-2427
http://www.inw.state.il.us

Indiana

Indiana Department of Insurance
311 West Washington Street, Suite 300
Indianapolis, IN 46204-2787
317-232-2385
http://www.in.gov/idoi/

Iowa

Iowa Insurance Division
330 Maple Street
Des Moines, IA 50319-0065
515-281-5705
877-955-1212
http://www.iid.state.ia.us

Kansas

Kansas Insurance Department
420 Southwest Ninth Street
Topeka, KS 66612-1678
800-432-2484
http://www.ksinsurance.org/

Kentucky

Kentucky Department of Insurance
215 West Main Street
Frankfort, KY 40601
800-595-6053
http://doi.ppr.ky.gov/kentucky/

Louisiana

Louisiana Department of Insurance
1702 North Third Street
Baton Rouge, LA 70802
800-259-5300
800-259-5301 (Louisiana only)
http://www.ldi.state.la.us

Maine

Maine Bureau of Insurance
124 Northern Avenue
Gardiner, Maine 04345
207-624-8475
http://www.maine.gov/pfr/insurance/

Maryland

Maryland Insurance Administration Agency
525 St. Paul Place
Baltimore, MD 21202-2272
800-492-6116
http://www.mdinsurance.state.md.us

Massachusetts

Massachusetts Division of Insurance
One South Station
Boston, MA 02110-2208
617-521-7794
617-521-7777 (consumer information hotline)
http://www.state.ma.us/doi

Michigan

Michigan Consumer and Industry Services
Office of Financial and Investment Services
Ottawa Building, Third Floor
611 West Ottawa
Lansing, MI 48933-1070
877-999-6442
http://www.michigan.gov/cis

Minnesota

Minnesota Department of Commerce
85 Seventh Place East, Suite 500
St. Paul, MN 55101
651-297-7161
http://www.commerce.state.mn.us

Mississippi

Mississippi Insurance Department
1001 Woolfolk State Office Building
501 North West Street
Jackson, MS 39201
800-562-2957
http://www.doi.state.ms.us

Missouri

Missouri Department of Insurance
301 West High Street, Room 530
Jefferson City, MO 65101
573-751-2640 (Jefferson City)
816-889-2381 (Kansas City)
314-340-6870 (St. Louis)
800-726-7390 (consumer hotline)
http://insurance.mo.gov

Montana

Montana State Auditor
840 Helena Avenue
Helena, MT 59601
800-332-6148
http://sao.state.mt.us

Nebraska

Nebraska Department of Insurance
Terminal Building
941 "O" Street, Suite 400
Lincoln, NE 68508-3639
http://www.state.ne.us/home/NDOI

Nevada

Nevada Division of Insurance
2501 East Sahara Avenue, Suite 302
Las Vegas, NV 89104
702-486-4009
http://www.doi.ne.gov/

New Hampshire

New Hampshire Insurance Department
56 Old Suncook Road
Concord, NH 03301-7317
603-271-2261
800-852-3416 (consumer assistance)
http://www.state.nh.us/insurance

New Jersey

New Jersey Department of Banking and Insurance
P.O. Box 325
Trenton, NJ 08625
609-292-5316
http://www.state.nj.us/dobi

New Mexico

New Mexico Public Regulation Commission, Insurance Division
P.E.R.A. Building
1120 Paseo De Peralta
P.O. Box 1264
Santa Fe, NM 87501
800-947-4722
http://www.nmprc.state.nm.us

New York

New York State Insurance Department
25 Beaver Street
New York, NY 10004
212-480-6400 (consumer services)

or
One Commerce Plaza
Albany, NY 12257
518-474-6600
http://www.ins.state.ny.us

North Carolina

North Carolina Department of Insurance
P.O. Box 26387
Raleigh, NC 27611
919-733-2032
800-546-5664 (consumer services)
http://www.ncdoi.com

North Dakota

North Dakota Department of Insurance
600 East Boulevard, Department 401
Bismark, ND 58505-0320
701-328-2440
http://www.state.nd.us/ndins

Ohio

Ohio Department of Insurance
2100 Stelles Court
Columbus, OH 43215-1067
614-644-2658
800-686-1526 (consumer hotline)
http://www.ohioinsurance.gov

Oklahoma

Oklahoma Insurance Department
P.O. Box 53408
Oklahoma City, OK 73152-3408
800-522-0071
http://www.oid.state.ok.us

Oregon

Oregon Insurance Division
350 Winter Street Northeast, Room 440
Salem, OR 97301-3883
503-947-7980
http://www.cbs.state.or.us/ins/

Pennsylvania

Pennsylvania Department of Insurance
Consumer Services
Room 1701 State Office Building
1400 Spring Garden Street
Philadelphia, PA 19130
215-560-2630
http://www.ins.state.pa.us/ins/site/default.asp

Rhode Island

Rhode Island Department of Business Regulation
23 Richmond Street
Providence, RI 02903
401-222-2246
http://www.dbr.state.ri.us

South Carolina

South Carolina Department of Insurance
300 Arbor Lake Drive, Suite 1200
Columbia, SC 29223
803-737-6160
https://www.doi.sc.gov/

South Dakota

South Dakota Division of Insurance
445 East Capitol Avenue
Pierre, SD 57501
605-773-3563
http://www.state.sd.us/drr2/reg/insurance

Tennessee
Tennessee Department of Commerce and Insurance
Davy Crockett Tower, Suite 500
Nashville, TN 37243-0565
615-741-6007
http://state.tn.us/commerce/

Texas
Texas Department of Insurance
P.O. Box 149104
Austin, TX 78719-9104
800-578-4677
800-252-3439 (consumer helpline)
http://www.tdi.state.tx.us

Utah
Utah Department of Insurance
State Office Building, Room 3110
Salt Lake City, UT 84114-6901
801-538-3800
800-439-3805 (Utah only)
801-538-3805 (consumer services)
http://www.insurance.utah.gov/

Vermont
Vermont Department of Banking and Insurance,
Insurance Division
89 Main Street, Drawer 20
Montpelier, VT 05620-3101
802-828-3301
http://www.bishca.state.vt.us/InsurDiv/insur_index.htm

Virginia

Virginia Bureau of Insurance
Tyler Building
1300 East Main Street
Richmond, VA 23219
804-371-9741
800-552-7945 (Virginia only)
http://www.scc.virginia.gov/division/boi/

Washington

Washington State Office of the Insurance Commissioner
P.O. Box 40255
Olympia, WA 98504-0255
360-725-7000
http://www.insurance.wa.gov

West Virginia

West Virginia Insurance Commission
1124 Smith Street
Charleston, WV 25301
304-558-3354
304-558-3386 (consumer hotline)
800-642-9004 (consumer hotline—West Virginia only)
http://www.wvinsurance.gov

Wisconsin

Wisconsin Office of the Commissioner of Insurance
125 South Webster Street
Madison, WI 53702
608-266-3585
800-236-8517 (Wisconsin only)
http://oci.wi.gov

Wyoming

Wyoming Department of Insurance
Herscher Building, Third Floor East
122 West Twenty-fifth Street
Cheyenne, WY 82002
307-777-7401
http://insurance.state.wy.us

About the Author

Ron is a consultant to the life insurance industry with an emphasis upon marketing. His areas of specialty include life settlements, estate planning, and premium finance solutions. He also works with many accounting and other financial services firms consulting in all aspects of marketing life insurance and life settlement products.

He is a noted author whose articles can be found in national publications such as The CPA Journal, The National Underwriter, The Journal of Accountancy, as well as many other regional and local publications. Most recently Ron has been consulting on a national basis with many insurance companies including Morgan Belle USA, a full service insurance organization.

Ron entered the life insurance business in 1988 upon graduation from The George Washington University, in Washington DC. He subsequently received his Chartered Life Underwriter (CLU) and Chartered Financial Consultant (ChFC) degrees from The American College, in Bryn Mawr, PA.

If you are interested in exploring your or your company's insurance, life settlement, estate planning, or marketing needs with Ron, he can be contacted at:

> Morgan Belle USA
> 21 Walt Whitman Road
> Huntington Station, NY 11746
>
> Tel: 631-424-2300
> Email: rroth@morganbelleusa.com

Index

www.ingramcontent.com/pod-product-compliance
Lightning Source LLC
Chambersburg PA
CBHW031056180526
45163CB00002BA/857